Thirty
Days

Anthologies from Tupelo Press

No Boundaries: Prose Poems by 24 American Poets
    edited by Ray Gonzalez

The Imaginary Poets
    edited by Alan Michael Parker

Myrrh, Mothwing, Smoke: Erotic Poems
    edited by Marie Gauthier and Jeffrey Levine

New Cathay: Contemporary Chinese Poetry
    edited by Ming Di

A God in the House: Poets Talk About Faith
    edited by Ilya Kaminsky and Katherine Towler

Another English: Anglophone Poems from Around the World
    edited by Catherine Barnett and Tiphanie Yanique,
    with Hinemoana Baker, Kwame Dawes, Ishion Hutchinson, Rustum Kozain,
    Les Murray, Sudeep Sen, and Todd Swift

Gossip and Metaphysics: Russian Modernist Poetry and Prose
    edited by Katie Farris, Ilya Kaminsky, and Valzhyna Mort

Thirty Days: The Best of the Tupelo Press 30/30 Project's First Year
    edited by Marie Gauthier

Thirty Days

THE BEST OF THE TUPELO PRESS
30/30 PROJECT'S FIRST YEAR

edited by Marie Gauthier

with a foreword by Kirsten Miles

T|P

TUPELO PRESS
North Adams, Massachusetts

Library of Congress Cataloging-in-Publication Data available upon request.
ISBN 978-1-936797-60-8

Cover and text designed by Howard Klein in Monotype Centaur.
Cover photograph: "Fishhouse" by Jeffrey Levine.

First paperback edition: April 2015.

Tupelo Press
P.O. Box 1767, 243 Union Street, Eclipse Mill, Loft 305
North Adams, Massachusetts 01247
Telephone: (413) 664–9611 / editor@tupelopress.org
www.tupelopress.org

Tupelo Press is an award-winning independent literary press that publishes fine fiction, nonfiction, and poetry in books that are a joy to hold as well as read. Tupelo Press is a registered 501(c)(3) nonprofit organization, and we rely on public support to carry out our mission of publishing extraordinary work that may be outside the realm of large commercial publishers. Financial donations are welcome and are tax deductible.

Contents

Foreword

The Tupelo Press 30/30 Project began with a conversation between Jeffrey Levine and Tupelo Press editor Cassandra Cleghorn, a well-published poet in her own right, who had suggested a novel, artistic approach to incubating poetry while simultaneously supporting a worthy cause. That idea was then shared with poet Rebecca Kaiser Gibson, who was tackling the problem of how to be productive and maintain a motivation to put pencil to page, and who had asked Jeffrey about inspirational writing projects.

Rebecca challenged herself to "run" a marathon, vowing to write a poem a day for a month, posting her works-in-progress daily and raising money through pledges for Tupelo Press in the process. Marie Gauthier designed an elegant online home for the project, and Rebecca ended the month with thirty poems, an active and engaged readership, and a lovely donation for Tupelo Press. She commented that the effort was satisfying but a little lonely, saying that it would be nice to write in the company of others.

In January of 2013, nine poets joined to form a new team of marathoners, and the project came alive. Throughout the following year, for thirty days every month, fresh poems emerged and were sent to Marie Gauthier, who read each poem, each day, curating the blog and maintaining the connection between press and poet.

Since that first month, more than a hundred and ten poets have bravely posted newly drafted poems on our public forum. I emphasize the bravery required to post raw work. We are astonished and humbled to hear this often repeated avowal: "I will never again question that I am a poet. I found myself provoked and lifted by the work of others, taking risks I wouldn't have taken on my own." That is the gift of the 30/30 trifecta: accompanied writing; the urgency of an immediate and public deadline; and the interchange between poet and reader/sponsor — such positive interplay, that sweetest of fuels.

We can see poets challenging themselves with increasing freedom as the month progresses, allowing the communion with other poets to influence their work. Meanwhile, the growing cadre of 30/30 alumni continues to share publication strategies and successes, exploring the expanding boundaries of digital publication, and providing a vibrant international community for one another.

We couldn't be more excited that this original vision has created such powerful, joyous, and affirming ripples through the literary community.

Collectively, the 30/30 Project has helped Tupelo Press strengthen its mission to find more homes for books, and with this anthology we pay homage to these poets and their talent, perseverance, and generosity.

—Kirsten Miles
National Director of the 30/30 Program, and Director,
Tupelo Press Teen Writing Center Charlottesville, Virginia

Thirty Days

Rebecca Kaiser Gibson

Yearning

One limb of tree, most likely oak
                              grown old
                    in storms knocked
into a pine
          tumbled over jutting rock,
                              dangles in decay.

Cleaning the forest is thankless
                    I'm told.
                    No one lifts twigs
off feather moss to let it breathe.

                              Or says a bird blown
                    beak into wind
imprints the sky,
                              is a raised instance of itself.

          Neither bird,
(make it a crow with flappy wings)
          nor nothing is there.

          Was truly
                    but would not stay.

T. M. De Vos

In the movies

There is always a pure one,
who bakes or saves children,
with clear skin and smocks in light colors.

The bad are knife-pleated, draped in ermine-faced women —
so many, they seem immortal:
whatever is done to them, they recover;
when the hero leaves, they disperse
like wasps over fallen sweets.

Who could live with the pure tyrants
who hold hands firmly, sleep light?
They are like children, always right:
they are the breastfeeders, the teachers,
they are walking with canes.
Their sacrifices are loud and rattling
as poltergeists. In their country,
only clean water and right-of-way,
the cabinet-air of safety.

SHANNON ELIZABETH HARDWICK

Francine Avoids Blood Oranges for the Sound They Make Inside Her

Francine believes in prophecies like one believes in the body, the sea. Not of myself, she writes, but over it. Not the whole of the ocean, she writes, but within it. Francine walks after dinner each night to reach her. The self, she writes, eats oranges. Not blood, veins, fruit. Francine believes in prophecies like one believes in swallowing. There's a field with wheat, she writes, then food to eat. There's a boy undressing then a fight. A monster in us, a fish. This is my wish, she writes, to become a prophecy — lonely, untouched.

LINDSAY ILLICH

WTF Dear Mister Chrysler

thank you, Sugar

right there with the big nasty contrails
of disaster behind me and

the loved the left the gone and
even Lord remember the shuttle

blowing up right there in front of us and
fireweed and anklebones and my

sweet son somewhere in the blue
and all of it right there bearing down

hard and not even knowing
where it was I was

going in the middle of
what have I done what

have I done and the sidewalk
was furious with people

right there on 42nd where Bryant Park
ends and the Public Library

begins right there
it was right there

I looked up
I looked up and everything stopped:

the fuck was my life
and I was answering it

Mike McGeehon

Street Magician, Pikes Place

It's a thread, she tells me
as we watch the red ball dart
from one slight hand to the other,

leaping through hoops, dancing
to the song croaked off key
by the old man in a worn suit

conjuring at the market. No,
I reply, it's long hours of labor
in front of a bedroom mirror,

a lifetime learning patter
and slights, making this simple
as breathing, tuning out the crowd

to string out wonder for a few
dollars here in the wet, working
smooth as a palmed penny.

JANIE ELIZABETH MILLER

Golden Egg

I packed a nature documentary for my nature retreat
      and confess only the metallic sheen of loss,
            the dew-paste of wristwatch, burnished womb.

Emperor penguins skid like ellipses on their deflated bellies, each
      dragging a species on its heels, single
            golden egg between its legs.

In the bathroom the splatter of a woman's dead eggs stain the wall,
      her cotton tampon soaked in blood,
            another golden month.

In the cranky refrigerator hollow sounds of a glacier recede
      into hallows distant as the dry cough of a goose
            pinned neatly into this story's pattern.

Outside,

copper lights intercept darkness, the forest flings
      prayer beads into my throat's empty plume
      that swallows rivers in a paper cup.

A coyote mutters with spit jowl, human hunting
      season and deer are ripe with wild thyme
         sprouting in clusters.

Sometimes my eyelids seize under poetry's cleave, whenever a god
      stirs the pot, or when raven
         cracks a nut in its throat.

When was the origin of confession? When did the river stop translating
      the stars? I look to the forest for myth and the

sleek bone of beak,

the skin of the sea gesturing for the white flagged boat to set the
         planet free. I once imagined a golden deer
                  resting its head on my shoulder, but

what I meant
         was that it saved me the way a story clings
                  so closely to life that you walk into it

and wish hard that it may teach us how to live.

NINA PICK

Analogy

A tone to a trumpet
Is a what to a body

A nostalgia a voice a
Room newly cleaned

A weed by the sea a
Remembered noon

A long glow a
Slow decay

All of the above A
B, C, and D

Or none
Just a sentence

Heard in sleep like a
Breath caught mid-air

The cold exhalation
Made visible in flight

✿ ✿ ✿

Now that anger
has shrunk

its shell open,
I crawl out

and see

our harvest,
turning.

So do you
in me.

So do I
in him.

We see.
We close our eyes,

still see.

End User License Agreement

This Poem is licensed to You, for use only under the terms of this license.

You may not rent or lease this Poem. You may not reverse engineer, disassemble, or attempt to derive the source code of this Licensed Poem, and revisions thereof.

You agree that the Poem may collect and use data and related information, including but not limited to information about Your interpretation, explication, extrapolation, or personal tastes.

You understand that by reading the Poem, You may encounter content that may be deemed offensive, indecent, or objectionable, which content may or may not be identified as having explicit language, and that the results of any exposure to the Poem may automatically and unintentionally generate ideas or references about other objectionable material. You agree to read the poem at Your sole risk, and that the Poet shall not have any liability to You for content that may be found to be offensive, indecent, or objectionable.

You agree not to use the Poem in any manner to harass, abuse, stalk, threaten, defame, or otherwise infringe or violate the rights of any other party, and that the Poet is not in any way responsible for any such use by You nor for harassing, threatening, defaming, offensive, or illegal messages or transmissions that You may receive as a result of reading this Poem.

The Licensed Poem is presented "As Is" and "As Available," with all faults and without warranty of any kind, and the Poet hereby disclaims all warranties and conditions with respect to the Licensed Poem, including but not limited to the implied warranties and/or conditions of marketability, of artistry, of satisfactory quality, of fitness for a particular purpose, of accuracy, of quiet enjoyment, that the License Poem will meet Your requirements, that the Licensed Poem will be error-free, or that the defects in the Licensed Poem shall be corrected.

In no event shall the Poet be liable for personal injury, or any incidental, special, indirect, or consequential damages whatsoever, including but in no way limited to damages for loss of profits.

You agree that You will not use this Poem for the development, design, manufacture, or production of nuclear missiles or chemical or biological weapons.

This license is effective until terminated by You or the Poet. Your rights under this license terminate automatically without notice from the Poet if You fail to comply with any of the terms of this license. Upon termination of the license, You shall cease all reading of the Licensed Poem.

The listening to or reading of this Poem constitutes agreement with the End User License terms and conditions.

Margaret Young

January Sketches

Portland, Maine — Beverly, Massachusetts

In the graveyard, a new snowman,
twig-mohawked, twig arms held wide.

In the kitchen, onions in brown bags
sprout green insistent curves.

Frederick Church's rosy lake-reflecting view
of Ktaadn: who's that in that corner?

Another painter showed the mountain shorn,
burned off to make views for a new hotel.

Cars trucks trains tankers roads bridges
riverflow puddleslick slidealong down.

The bay's old name stays on the boats
linking the mainland to its islands.

I love you more than the Spud Trooper, a Star Wars-
themed Mr. Potato Head in the comic store is cool,

more than the distance between non-philosophy
and potatoes mashed with wild greens and milk.

ALISON CIMINO

From the Tree Line of Juniper

A crow emerges

fast flying low

robins squawk

flap wings   cry out.

But the crow flies

far over the field

leaves them

egg round and whole in its beak.

So the robins suffer while the crows delight —

but to see it —

bright blue sky

vast space

jet black body

an oval egg

perfect blue pearl

clutched   tender in its mouth.

Kate DeBolt

Cameraman

She saw me seeing and it was
all right, okay? Just upside down.

I'm a complicated puzzle.
I'm finding new ways

of opening the door, of answering
the phone. I approach them

crab-legged, with sideways steps.
Only grab the receiver between rings.

Pretend the knob is hot iron.
Both my hands are branded.

I can't tell anyone about the space
between my bed and wall,

where her ghost sits up nights
and purrs like an engine.

When I look at a screen,
the space between the cursor and her.

Just inverted.

In my iris she's upside down.
The tears roll back like Roman shades;

I freeze this frame.
The more things change.

Red-cheeked, lonely. Shame-faced
with too much table service

for a single cup of tea.

LENÉ GARY

an origin story

winter dreams
of sinking, of a sun
he can't resist
even if he knows
he'll lose himself
entirely, at least
for a while
he dreams of
sinking into every pore
of the earth, every
fissure in bark
he feels turtles begin to
stir and the warm bellies
of mice snow tunneling
the breath of birds
hunkered down in the cloud
of him and he wants to be
that close, that surrounded, that safe
in someone else. so he
dreams of spring
even if it means
the death of him, because
the rush of the river, the
scales of fish
brushing the night-
warming water
are too much for even
winter, even snow,
even the cold hard
world to say no, to
say no to, to the stretch

of roots, to the honey-
scent of twinflowers, no
to the soft scratch of herons'
feet, of crabs marking the mud

when it grows quiet long enough

even winter craves
   the song of spring
and in his dreaming, begins
calling her in

T. J. JARRETT

How Poems Work in Movies

In which there is crepuscular sun, and a field, or an ocean
we wade through, waist-deep. Unlike our world,

there is neither paper nor pen nor solitude here,
but the beloved, the gaze of the beloved,

words springing forth — resonant, in key.
The world we know still so new to us that it demands

abridged explaining: do not tell us how we pick up words
only to put them down again. Do not tell us of our doubts;

of doubt we could go on and on and on. Tell us the three things
we care about. Tell us our loss, longing and triumph —

succinctly and in that order. When you turn as you must,
return the bodies of our beloved to our gaze.

Give them back while they can still be saved.

JACEY BLUE RENNER

Sorrow Leaves the Body by Ox Cart

Bits of moss & rye, mixes of healthy
earth & chipped wood, damp mushroom.
There is a moment, when the dry last
leaves fall from the oaks, resin collecting
at the base of every last old growth.

The delicacy of time shatters with each Penelope sunrise.

And while every thing has begun
to curl away, loose, like tape
dried from the storage of past
conversations with ballpoint pens,
this nest of crows in my gut simply strains.

I want to squeeze the stars until they weep.

Or until they tell us how to mend the holes.
How to remix souls with salted waters
& grow sweet sweet peas from oleander ash.

Cranes teach us how to fold, into our creases, peace.

We pencil in ways to make the math
work. Around the edges we forget to erase
the things that made us wolves & strong,
able to handle the muscles hanging in our shops,
on the frames of our ribs. The heart beats:
petrification. The heart beats, woolen & pilled.

Ox after ox after oxen. Swish & spray of tale.

William David Ross

Cain's Departure

I took the toaster with its crumbs,
The Brazilian plates,
The t-shirts from their popup, fifth-wheel, & finally RV camper vacations,
The metal & the plastic toolboxes:

The tools —
The newly purchased razor-sharp chisels,
The ratchet-socket wrench sets, the sledgehammers, the levels, the wood &
    metal files,
The circular saw;

The socks,
The burgundy oxfords from Phil's in Essex Junction,
The pinewood shoebox with rags, polish, beeswax weatherproofing, &
    horsehair buffing-brushes,
The boots, Red Wing & steel toed;

The flannel button-up shirts,
The checkerboard (classic red & black) hunting pants,
The worn & pilled long johns,
The Ross plaid tie;

The *Spem Successus Alit* family crest pin with its fisted hand thrusting a laurel of
    juniper scale leaves,
The drop-leaf table,
The secretary desk, the walnut end table,
The wedding china they never used;

The black, veined leather & gold-leafed onionskin *Collected Writings of Wm.
    Shakespeare* he rescued from the landfill,
The botany & the bird books from 1956,
The paintings — Impressionist & Baroque posters really —

The regal, hangnail brushstrokes of light dying eyes in Rembrandt's 1669,
   last *Self-Portrait*;

The cyclocross bike we bought together that glows in the dark, the well-used
   & still taut catgut snowshoes,
The wide-leg sweatpants —
The last pants he wore I've sentimentally placed over
The last pants she wore;

Yet, I left
The hope of all kin behind there, nodded to
The red ranch sold where they'd spent thirty-seven years just a fraction of a
   degree above the dead-end,
The zero, the full plummet of the mercury-thermometer-bottom-round-bulb
   cul-de-sac;

I left
The claret clapboard house that wholly entombs
The dual Cain guilty & adopted sons' of my parents & another questionable
   brood of their union —
The mute & sexless mock-love sadly forged marriage;

I left
The gospel truth of them now barely kept incarnate & lingering from
The shroud cast by what once we did or we did not do there at 23
   Cobbleview Drive that promises to resurrect
The razed, to recall our taken & left & utterly dismembered family.

JOANNA SOLFRIAN

If Ever I Would Leave You

How to remain gentle, with the gods overthrown like that.
It's been a couple of months since the disaster,
and you hear a woman say, by means of soothing,
"God wanted the best angels," a statement with such mastery
of denial you almost retch. God does not select
his own society at the ample expense
of ours. But let's examine the nature of the phrase
"a couple of months" — there are those who know
precisely the number of days and who will always know
precisely the number of days. They were beautiful.
They drew yellow suns with stick arms and skies
that never touched ground.
But what if your own soul is so dismal a rising
that you cannot bear this woman and her god?
At night, you watch the old tape, shot
at a fundraiser. Your father sings from Camelot,
Oh, no, not in springtime, and your mother
accompanies, nine months from sod,
dying in scraps of the disease you're fundraising to fight.
For such a forward-dripping thoughtless sap,
time is stutteringly redundant.
Over and over again, it's *no, never could I leave you at all* . . .
and over and over again you pray for the night
to reverse itself. You, and the others.
But then it's a couple more months, the green ribbons tatter,
and even you must hum at the world's ancient craft, the daffodils'
first spires. The square jaw on t.v. talks Affordable Care,
and your neighbor with the Subaru takes down her sign
and the twenty stapled teddy bears.

Dan Thomas-Glass

28s (Creeley) XXVI

Relative to cost, the high figures
of production:
you, sweetness & light
are destructive only in your
inveterate tendencies. Bright
copper economies
strip sun colors from phones
sun of its color
where the dead birds whirr.
Tables to count costs
in bodies:
relative sweetness of precise
strikes cauterize
daytime. Old old old
our bones betray us.
Today the book
said the owl's house
had owl feathers
& Alma nodded her head
with the babies
yeah
wanting mommy
to read the book again. High
in the trees those
other feathers & other bones:
dead fish in the eagle's nest.
Our naked bodies shine
bomber engines in the sun.

NINA ISRAEL ZUCKER

The Divorce

She sat on the edge of my beach towel
to tell me about her year. How she divorced
her husband and married her college boyfriend.
They found each other, I don't remember how,
perhaps on Facebook. She said, he is my lucky third.
Three is the magic number I say. I ask about
her children, if they were upset, and she says, oh yes
they are very upset with me. They love their stepfather.
They love their father. And then she said, I don't even mind
that he smokes cigars and has a big belly. I do what I want.

We do what we want. If everything really follows a pattern,
like a flower, like the lines on the back of the woodpecker,
black, white, black, white, if the rocks really are alive,
if the police officer stops to ask me if I need help
because I have been sitting outside in my car for an hour
and someone called with concern, fear that I might be
planning to break in. What could I steal? That marriage
is over, that wave is in. Summer or no summer, we wait
for the boys to come out and join us under the trees,
or by a lake, or in the never, ever.

Serena Chopra

[untitled]

The mothers are awaiting you, they took to you

like spears, resemble draped cane-shadows

and speak chrome to your muted eyes.

> The cool approach vanishes

> like a child.

An echo performs the obligations

of darkness —

The work to be done here takes fine tools,

slim arrangements of muscle fiber —

> *The weaving is done as the fabric grows dense.*

The cells here

are blind.

JILL CRAMMOND

Mary Goes Below the Surface

for Diana McGrath

Frozen lake, after sunset, across a sheet of ice,
Mary searches for the other women.
All her life she has tried to fit in,
worn beautiful robes,
whispered sweetened prayers,
feasted on suitors and saviors.

She has heard it is a different world
down below: slick of seaweed between the legs,
thick lips and silken scales,
mermaids for wet nurses,
fine ocean views.

Like most virgins, Mary believes she is stalking the divine,
forgets her swimsuit, her air tank,
her bright orange life vest.
She is on her own in this sprawl of spawning mothers,
absent men and sand.

The hole so easy to cut,
the dive so easy to make.
Tip of the blade and rhythm,
pointed toes and thrust.

Oh Shanty Town,
Oh Lonely Bride,
Oh One that Got Away,
what your net can't hold on land,
is the very thing that will kill you here.

Rachel Fogarty-Oleson

Cicatrix

my face is wood
I never look up, only grow
older with eyes
the color of an ants wing: pale
my mouth is a scar
left in a house for years;
turned into a doorstep
measures meant to be corrected
my hair a confetti of ashes
its thinness crackles
like a winter's cabin: I want to
be that first fallen snow, and remember
nothing

BRETT ELIZABETH JENKINS

Suite for Lost Loves (in D Minor)

I.
My heart's dialect twanged slow
and southern around you and sometimes,
without notice, it still says the word *why*
like baby's too-long wail: *wah.*

II.
You are the one who taught me to play chess,
and the meaning of wisteria, namely the dark girl
who steps out of the painting and offers
herself to a man, shoeless, her hair able to blow in the wind,
and she can imagine her life among people with full legs
and sweeping arms, and trees that bend and bend and bend.

When she steps back into the painting, I'm sure,
the saltwater is streaked and blown dry
by the wind she can only see now.

III.
And the French verb for *confess.*

IV.
You wind-wheeled from the tip
of a faraway bridge,
and tonight I will dream you
return to me as a goose
coming in low and hard
with your beak just
skimming the surface
of the river.

KALI LAMPARELLI

The Docks

When you arrive there from here, you think
you can go home again.
Travel on route 24 past old mill buildings
windows shattered in. Lose yourself at 114
car after car.
Find the natural conclusion, the ocean beating
the sand out in front of you. You need this beauty.
The coast winds itself between gilded mansions
lifetimes that shadow the streets and hang people
with tours and smiles. History is deadly.
Bring only what you know. Nights you'll spend at the docks
throwing cut-up photos of him off the edge. Wishing you could
drown him for emptying you here.

poem, poem

my beard is a shapeless donkey the plastic wig of
my beard struts its skeletal strut
my beard grows a lake in the reeds you can hear
my beard growing a landscape inside me
my beard grows a tree of wind in me
my beard walks on four legs the birth of
my beard grows its roots in me yesterday
my beard drowned itself in the river. the hunger of
my beard is not a beard across the river a crow
my beard is the ocean the sky. the dirt of
my beard tears a glass eye of rain. in the mirror
my beard is a charlatan. in the shadows of
my beard a shaman is chanting. the house of
my beard walks on all fours today and today and today
my beard sets itself on fire

LUISA MURADYAN

One Bird at a Time

There is an instructor who gives his students perfect scores
on their exams if they answer every question incorrectly
and I think this is a test of divinity
because accuracy will turn you into an insect.
Remembering that wild hour where
two plus two equaled zero
crawling to the front of the classroom in your cargo shorts
as the others chanted zero
a zero in your mouth where there was once a tongue.
Your wings open, your body shed its exoskeleton
a naked zero standing against the blackboard.
A zero between the G and D, is it a naked number that
makes language holy?

*

And I think about the first person who invented zero.
Hands cupped together watching the water
escape through her fingers
or the man who was given one hundred oxen
and watched each one walk into the wilderness
or about those who no longer want a body
and believe in zero,
clouds in the shape of zero,
the sun a burning zero,
the earth holding nothing but zero
and for one minute
the moon makes us believe
in fullness.
as they take turns
flying off of a building

and we stand there
saying goodbye
one bird at a time.

DAN NOWAK

wishful sonnet about snow

i've stopped watching the snow because i keep thinking it isn't going to
melt if i do, some sort of reverse boiling, some sort of wishful osmosis.
i keep picturing a land that doesn't open its jaws up to this gentle assault
rom the sky. i think these moments are less and less about me. i think of
throwing all of my life outside and seeing if that will stem the clouds
as if i were the omen, if i were misery's doppelgänger. then i make snow
angels. beautiful naked things on the ground, unable to be anatomical
and wishful that i hadn't just sat on them. i cover my pants in awkward
camouflage and wish it were all just cameo. there are no more word ups,
no more wishes than the next person walking their pug in a silly little coat
on the street. i share the same ground with that pup peeing and i should
want for only that. everything else is a false Christmas, everything else
makes me think there is something more and more even if there is not.

Emily R. Rudofský

Did Don Juan Eat Like This?

The sign says, EAT OYSTERS, LOVE LONGER.
The young and green, the old and mad
with mouths of silt and brine — hope of tantric bliss.

Elsewhere men drink cobra blood in sherry glasses
and toss their little wives all night.
Elsewhere nosy neighbors give young couples
roasted and sugared gossamer wings and spindle legs —
then listen through the wall.

When you ate wine-soaked water lilies
you forgot falling asleep on your back with a sigh of defeat —
just wind through the pyramids.

Eat slugs, slow and moist as glue.
Feed them to each other like birds,
until so full you cannot fly.
Bodies painted in the slime of love.

Justin Boening

How I Came to Rule the World

First, no one loved me. Then I loved myself
too much. The rest, as they say, is the rest.
I ran and ran for what seemed like months,
through a stampede of bulls, the inferno
one is promised and always dreams of.
I prayed for god to take me
until he did. At the edge of a city
I stopped at a bus-stop and sat there —
I removed my clothes:
                    The wind swelled,
I pulled off a boot; some fog dissolved,
I flung my hat into the street. Then a woman
rushed down the boulevard of ash, between
rows of bare-limbed trees, and her endless
wailing dispersed through the corridor
of empty parking lots:
                  "You have forgotten to pay me
and have forgotten the medicine I need
to nurse you back to health."
                  I couldn't believe her.
I rode her bicycle wearing nothing but a scarf
quickly as I could to the center of the city, a piazza
of black marble and black trees growing like wire
from the marble, and there emerged, its bronze
curves rusted, flaked in mint lichen, right there
within the muggy vicinity, a statue of me.
And I wept beneath it on my knees, relieved
at its being there but mostly tired
of the punishment. And that was it.
How I came to rule the world? It was easy.

FLOWER CONROY

Our Lady of UV—A Light

O
ma-
donna,
mothership
of deep purple
filter material, arms
outstretched, poised
neon tangerine lips: tonite
we bathe in the trance that is
your stroboscopic liquid ice &
licorice light fountain. Haloed
in mercury vapor, atomic emitting
diodes, your green eyes sear in retinal
raving, your bug zapper turquoise light-
ning blessings juice us up. Patron Saint
of tanning beds, skittles nettle our skin. O
coruscated in sweat & fairy dust, all fox fire
& photon, the Deejay's never-ending sick beats
infuse me with your majesty. Uranium blooded,
you are all forensics & fluorescence. Virtuous Rock
Huntress, Illuminati of Ringworm & Counterfeit $$$,
your electrolier bombilation, hypnotic as the flamboyant
nimbus bass delights your followers — we are ecstatic.
Some writhe, some bask in your underwater static &
thrum in cuddle-puddles. Lamp, Eminence, in
your wake, all other razzlematazz pales. You
suspend time in your House of Ware, this
vacant tomb of floors & exposed beams.
O let your wicked wick sputter enlight-
enment upon me that I may peak &
gaze upon the face of heaven —
paparazzi flashes of Christ-
mas tree & mirror ball,
glitter, tinsel & rain-
bow trails flick-
ering back
at me.

LISA DeSIRO

Hawks in Harvard Square

Sometimes they hover, sometimes glide
above the buildings. Citified,
they perch atop the church clock
tower, or the high-rise by the park —

that park where once I thought something
swept past in a blur, swooping
into the plane tree nearest me.
But from underneath all I could see

was quivering greenish sunlight twisted
between branches. The hawks had nested
only in my mind. No matter.
Wind went rippling like dry water

through their feathers, through my hair,
through the air throughout the square.

HOLLY DAY

Housewarming

We fill our home with mismatched groves
of pine and oak and molded plastic chairs,
put monogrammed napkins
at every place setting. The scientists come
right on time to study our relationship, offer
kind, unwelcome comments as we pass

plates laden with meat and cheese,
refill their glasses with wine.
This one is my father, that one is your mother,
there are others, too.
They exchange notes, compare findings,
shake their heads and sigh
at something incurable, intangible, inconsolable.

We make excuses: for the furniture
the condition of the house
for the awkward weather
for each other.
Later, in the dark, I feel the scatter
of scars on your skin
try to read their dents of Braille graffiti
the broken ribs and puckers
that catalog all the unmet longings. This place

will never smell like home, just as you
will never be completely naked around me. In the end
you will leave me
howling, all alone, at the moon.

Naoko Fujimoto

Unnatural Violence

My father had never slapped anything.

Even he did not kill a long-legged wasp
carrying spring dirt from the field.

He poked it with a flyswatter and said,
Please leave, Mr. Bee ...

My mother said,
Kill it now,

and brought insecticide.

We used to live on the fifteenth floor,
but we occasionally had wasps.

My sister and I dropped things like
dolls, colored pencils,

and gumballs over the balcony.

Sometimes these things
stayed in one piece.

When we could not find the doll's left arm,
we climbed up a fence

in the dark quadrangle.

There was a small wreath.

We looked up at the building

and saw a narrow

square of gray sky.

My sister asked,
Did someone jump?

We quickly recited a Buddhist sutra and ran.

MOLLY SUTTON KIEFER

Hush

When she says *Please mama, hush*, she is not asking
for quiet but song. She does not mean the sucking of boats
at shore or the falcon's measured wing. She does not mean
feather or wet snow or moon as it rises. Not:
the casual greeting of strangers in sleepy hallways
or the lung's last breath, the sound at the center of a storm
or the rest in a symphony. She does not mean
the quiet ease of blister, or the travel
of a blue bottle on the ocean. Not the surprise of
a sudden disappearance, the skiff of aurora borealis,
the ghost in the parlor, looking on. Not — the halo
of a sun dog or the holding of a secret. She does not mean
the rolling boil of water on the stove. The wishes you make
at the new year. Cusps and lisps. The steam let loose
from the bowl of winter soup; the space around stanzas.
She does not mean late night summer rain, the slick sound
of tires on pavement before the sun rises or autumn's
leaves shuttering to the ground. And too, she
doesn't know to cringe yet from my tone or shirk
from my breath in the morning. She insists,
Please, mama, sing a song. In this, she means —
my warble, that first lullaby, the one I gave her
when we spent nights in the living room and were full of offerings:
the croon of birds and spangle of diamond rings.

KATE LUTZNER

Snow

There is no poetry here, in the grass. Stark and unforgiving,
something I once failed to paint. The girl at work and I have
things in common. There are days I do not have a past,
like a new bird. I have forgotten what there is to hate.
My mother said never to use that word. The hub of people
forgetting my name is growing. Do not mistake that for pity.
I wanted to use the word *hub*. I don't have a child growing
out of its clothes. An ex-boyfriend had a baby yesterday
and I didn't even obsess over it. Thank you, Facebook,
for allowing me to prove myself. I will tell my husband
the good news. I will talk to him about snow, and carrying
the dog on the subway. Everyone mistook the dog for a cat.
He was in the vintage fabric-covered bag, small as a biscuit.
I could feel his heart beating, weak and fast.

DIANA KHOI NGUYEN

Shades of White

She stands in the background in order to be seen,
      like a door,
open,
      so that another door is seen.

      She is standing in this corridor
of shut doors,
      the color of a blood-filled creature,
nascent celebrity

dissolving
      like wafer on her tongue.

A hothouse flower exceeds the brilliance
      of even the brightest artificial light,

      like a hotelier's child
watching guests
from underneath the dining cart

      living in a diorama of her own life.
Doors open,
      they close. Through the scrim

      of pale curtains receding like a tide,
      like silk slipping off
the marbled ledge,

      an ivory gull leaves its wintering
to perch upon one
      tenterhook,

its missing yellow-tipped beak
       sleeping mindlessly inside its crop.

Listen:
       both the girl's song
and the bird's song are the same:

       cut-glass
       filling with rose water,
       joy
              netted on the underside
       of a wing.
            The song goes:

          I am the son.
   I am not the son.

MELISSA REESER POULIN

The Sweet and Disappearing

I remember talking to the sea, but not
what I said.

Somewhere, a woman hushes and lifts a singing kettle.
A child is born, a child dies.

A father is born, a father dies.
Boats rock in countless harbors.

Snow drifts, and so do petals, brushing
our eyelids and our paved streets.

I am comforted, I am unkind.
A prayer slips through the city like a needle trailing thread.

My friend comes out on the porch with her hands lifted,
two small, pink shells.

Meanwhile the ocean opens its mouth
far away from the throat of the river.

I open my mouth to ask
if it matters what I say.

Is it the want
or the wanting — to be useful — to be filled

with the weight of sameness, the level ache of need — empty
of questions?

I ask the sea,
whose sentence goes on for miles.

MARGIE SKELLY

Anatomy of a Woman

HAIR

Pull it back with your fingers,
satin before sheets,
remember its color in dawn, in twilight.

FOREHEAD

It appears as the beginning,
the start of the electric descent
to her body.

LIPS

Meet yours, man, a first impression,
so kiss her like a dancer —
deft, deliberate, decisive.

EYES

More than window panes or guides
reflections of her ancestral seeing
into childhoods of tomorrow.

SHOULDERS

Let your hands stop here.
Pause, like a comma,
before you touch gold.

Mattie Quesenberry Smith

Fibonacci Found It

It is spring on House Mountain,
And I am wondering how
Fibonacci found it
And believed that it matters,
That sequence of numbers
Hinging on what precedes them,
Running this springtime show.
Soon spring will be sanguine,
Shouting from steep shadows,
And the eight-petaled bloodroot,
A robust and pure lion
Rooted in his bloody rhizome,
Is a rare know-it-all.
A leaf encircles his stem.
Its strange, veined palm
Shields him from blood's loss.

M. Clara White

from Sailor's Knots

THE GRANNY

We decide, after all, that the brain is a collection,
a family of knots — those that center the roses
in a whimsy quilt, those that collapse to secure,

and some like a fist coiled in the brain. We decide
memory is only this: the unwrapping the rewrapping
in one day of a knot. First the ears like a rabbit's, then

the loop and squeeze. Remember how we tie the laces?
It slips inside itself, reverses, yes like aging —
How we never stay as we are made.

KATY CHRISLER

Wives and Children

When the barn burned
we called what was left
a moon house. Light
shone thru where windows
were as phantoms
left behind. Like the structure
just needed to breathe more.
Needed to let the life
that dwelt inside it out
into the field beside.
I often think of owls
and wonder what happened
to the small family
that lived in the rafters.
A small family of wives
and children and hope
they made it out to pasture.

CHRISTINE STARR DAVIS

Fewer Bees Now

after Antonio Machado

The impossibility of their flight,
the way their feet slide

inside the channels of crop blossoms
and emerge furred with agronomic

bullion. How heedless we shrug
off our weight of un-honeyed failures

and the bees' retreat, eye-roll
headlines that trumpet the hives'

vacancies. Listen. The crops talk
in the paucity of shoots. They tell us.

DONELLE DREESE
Mind Balloon

I'm no shrinking violet!
    Overheard in a hallway
        that was not a garden.

Good to know, but are you the corpse flower
    largest of all flowers, rare as ghost orchids
        but smells of rotting flesh

    are you consciousness expanding
        a well-kneaded intellectual bread batter
            slowly bubbling and browning over the side
        of the baking dish

    or a mind balloon over-puffed and wind-inflated
        with hot gusts, its translucent thin skin
            showing psyche stretch marks?

I wonder if you are sorry
    for the aggressive crop-dusting
        if you've ever tried decaf?

I have a safety pin in my pocket.
I'm not the only one.

ALAN KLEIMAN

Sunny Day

The elephant sat awkwardly
on his hind legs
his trunk waving in the air.
Giddyap he thought
but he didn't say a word.
The sky was blue
the grass green
and peanuts still under
$3 a pound unshelled.
Don't get me started
on shelled peanuts
or dry roasted.
It's important not to pollute
an elephant's thoughts
on a summer day in spring.
They know the difference
Just like you and me.

DESMOND KON ZHICHENG-MINGDÉ

x is for xyst

because walking under the world canopy
is as liminal as this rite of passage
of the written as language as pavement
as cobbled walkway as history as
authenticity as unintended as onerous
as ominous as opulent and promising
as the new and the endless portico of marble
walter benjamin walking in his arcades
with whitman again in a cart without wheels
like a lost charioteer with a big hat
driving himself steady against what resists
like zeno and another perplexing puzzle
about life and how it's trapped yet soaring
into the atlas and annals of time

BARBARA MARCH

Spell Check Penelope or the Oleputian Muse Never Sleeps

Monk's sandals in a daisy chain
flow like cream, nag me, nag me,
write yes, sleep no.

Late night words
clog my pen like pine needles
my neighbor stuffs in the weir.

A poem stings my hand.
Spell check Penelope lopes ole, ole,
here and there on the note pad.

Glasses on, glasses off,
words roll behind my eyes
smooth as stones we throw

in the ditch where the water
spills over the edge.
Oh, all right, two pillows, two pills.

21 days into 30
I'll write you;

broccoli stalk, frozen bears,
oranges, oranges, toupee, swamp tree.

COLIN POPE

Eating Grapes

Well, here's one more machine
I don't know how to operate.
One end will get you drunk. The other
is a sunny day. On the front steps.
And there's a bowl filled
with light and woody vines.
The cars are going by and you
are sitting, head leaned back
into your mother's chest, just
watching. It's almost I'm done
with my grapes can I go play? But
not quite. They're gone, one by one,
and more than sweetness, more
than skin clinging to teeth, I feel
water. Running through my hands
to clean, to move as if it knew
where it was going, as if
it had always known
and the fruit, the sun,
the memory, everything
had only gotten in the way.

ARLO VOORHEES

A Sonnet for the Millennials

It's not a bore
to think creat-
ively; ignore
your status update,
your digital
photo feed,
so literal-
ly you'll re'd-
iscover
imagination
or a lover's
declaration.
A scroll will not suffice.
You'll have to read this twice.

SALLY FISHER

Dickinson's Windows

We had made a reservation
because people lived there.

Smells from the kitchen climbed the stairs.
The house was alive.

Her room is spare, perhaps not stylish even then.
The sleigh bed looks almost Roman.

Our guide pulls the white dress from the closet, on a hanger.
Holes pierce the neck where a brooch was pinned, unpinned, pinned.

An iron stove stands before the west window
where winter's afternoon sky burns red as coals.

I think of her stoking that stove
her bedroom heading west like a train

not toward her brother's house where all had turned
cruel, but west past the house, the town, the sky.

In the morning she sits near the south window, folds her papers,
pierces them like the dress, sews them together, needle and thread.

LOIS P. JONES

Colony Collapse Disorder

It is impossible to tell a lie under the linden.
— German folklore

Under the blooming linden
we whorled across a morning

a lattice of furred bodies
striped with sun and hunger.

Bellies trembling for honey crop
we drank what was given, trusting

its wave of nectar — branches dripping
with sap. And the air thrummed

in urgency something like a chant
as we pressed our mouths

in the milk-faced florets
balancing on a tight rope

of slender stalks. Anyone
watching would see how we bent

like dozing children, tipsy
from a sip of wine. How

in a normal world we would fly
home to relinquish the weight

of our sacks to the rest
of the hive — run our mandibles

through sticky combs left to right
urging the others to return.

Anyone could witness the quick
vertigo. How we tumbled to the dirt

struggling for a moment
on our backs as if a sudden wind

had dropped our bodies
in a field of dark fruit,

as if we'd found sustenance
there.

Janet Kenning

Hopscotch

Federico Garcia Lorca hears his heart beating at five
In the afternoon. Something changes.
He hammers stars into the evening sky. One by one
They appear and make the night grow black.
Dostoevsky climbs dark apartment stairs in Petersburg,
Remembers the firing squad, the reprieve. Startles awake
Cursing loneliness, a bright sun on a white night.
Keith Richards watches the wall, his shadow
Touching wallpaper, a song in his head,
Pepper vodka in a plastic cup.
A journalist in Sarajevo … crouched behind a jeep
As his best friend bleeds in the street. An airline ticket
Falls from the pocket of his camo jacket, hands begin
To tremble as the shots stick in the stone wall at his back.
And the angel they seek draws a few boxes with chalk,
Throws a little stone and starts to count.
From an open window in the house next door, she hears
Someone play a cello. She stops to take
A little breath, smiles ever so slightly.
Step, step, jump.

JACQUELINE KOLOSOV

On the Ways in Which June Differs from August

June is daylight's furthest reach,
August — a wearied sentinel
following the sun, or the shadows of our bare-
skinned children lengthening on the lawn.
June's the seedlings' becoming — such deep-marrow
pleasure in the first eggplant's blossoming,
and now the cherry tomatoes are putting forth stars.
August is watermelon anticipating apples,
afternoon's humid sleep. And June?
The child's plunge into the chlorinated
blue, each ripple as supple as this evening's
primrose, your hand-in-mine, our footsteps
oh-so-quiet on the path. August's the mind's
leap across sixty-some tomorrows,
each one chanted in the jump rope's *one-two*
rhythm of sticky cheeks and fingers, knees skinned,
grass-stained, and dusted with sidewalk chalk.
All real living is meeting, Martin Buber said, *and prayer
is not in time, but time in prayer,*
the hands becoming steeples, trees, towers
for containing the echoes, a mountain
that remembers the pilgrim's journey
along the path. Yes,
time's hands are vessels hallowing
the butterfly's wing, but also the moth's.
Always remember the fervor of each
moonlit being's insistent tremor —

Five

One learned to swim alone at night
in a shallow pond, splashing brown
water and sycamore leaves until she
buoyed.
        Another grew lilies taller
than her child had been, and bright
yellow.
        Another carried salt in her pocket
in case of need.
        Another moved stones from place
to place and found this changed nothing.
        The last one walked, so she could tell
those who asked how she planted her feet
and peeled them from the earth, how each
step holds both greeting and farewell.

J. Kirk Maynard

I. vii. [knock-on effect]

Day break : she builds each piece just as she planned,
sanded symmetrical, twice measured
once cut : shim of miter's teeth to weathered
wood, her handiwork is within her hands,

clamped down. And made in cautious measurements
the act of cutting, planning, painting at,
a wordless charge in such a noisy silence sat
and myself tasked to rhyming temperaments.

Which is the source of our knock-on effect?
The words I write where no-sense sounds are kept,
or how her work becomes screwed, jigged, and sealed?

From hand to hand our work's perpetual,
— one's real, the other's conceptual —
marking twice what's only once revealed.

Heidi Johannesen Poon

Nystagmus

The eye goes back and forth
until the room turns on its violated hip.

Dizziness heightens now
that it's on the stage like a snake:

pig nosed and full of conditions.
The doctor, taking hold of the head,

snug against his chest like the pedestal itself.
Getting up slowly from identity —

the vertiginous eye envies its own name —
to soak up what's cared for,

importuned with the best of us,
bittering in company it cannot keep.

Lisa Donne Sampson

Chemistry lessons at the beginning of a life

for Sarah Ann Vannozzi

Swirl of numbers and design, C.E. '65, Sarah's born
astral, rational as shell and pearl
raised atom by particle and meant to change what we mourn —
available light on objects found,
half-life of roses tightly bound. A conch

Appressed to their lips, poets in '67 blew a kiss to the
New Frontier athanor that launched a
neverland, apres-vous. Her globed retorts amassed, her own

vanguard attached, at age two she defends the laws of science.
At the nadir in '68, the Sergeant Pepper Age,
now three, she knows her giants are
non-violent, but carry the strain of right spent wrong,
overhanging all these pendant stars, beckoning from the
zenith astir with super-nova chemistry; her child's faith secure inside a
zebrawood box lined with the certain fabric of a day when her life is
inscribed as she knows it to be — the thermodynamic balance of light and energy.

LARISSA SZPORLUK

Bull Mountain

Innate goodness strays.
You run after your chickens,
but not your good feelings.

These apricot trees
were under the sea once.
The sea had to die

for land to have chickens.
Beginnings are bald.
Your father's old legs

drag through the water,
so like the water
that no one is in them.

Risa Denenberg

On the morning of the second day

After the word was first uttered (during that one-way
conversation you later can't remember) you suddenly
know (an odd word, because everything uncertain is)
that it has seeded or mutated or whatever it is cancer does,
and there you are, joined with a myth of creation.

THIRD DAY, NOON

Goddamn fucking cancer! Freakish beast, arising from the ether
of your breast, your prostate, your colon, your liver, your very
bones, these private plummy places you've never once offered
up to it. And we who share your species affirm: *so unfair,*
so young, so gifted, so promising.

FIFTH DAY, 3 AM

Without remorse, it has latched on like a suckling pig
to your cells and won't let go. This bioform (size of a fist)
from some other phylum started out smaller than a sperm,
invisible without pricy machinery; and let's face it,
those experts with their fancy PET scans missed it anyway.

ON THE SEVENTH DAY, WHILE GOD IS BUSY RESTING

It shoves and pushes, gobbling calories, imbibing marrow.
Everything you hate about lodging this gatecrasher will be

conflated by its treatment, a rageful act of warfare that will, like cancer itself, shove its profligate eye into your household and oust everything from the garden you once called you.

JANET RUTH HELLER
Spring, 2013

Cold winds blew
in April, May, and June,
freezing the cherry blossoms
but sparing the apples and rhubarb.

In July, rain fell often,
fattening the black raspberries
and thrusting the daylilies
five feet above the ground.

Today, the rose of Sharon
in our front yard
burst into bloom,
white petals with a blood-red heart.

All-Points Bulletin

Do we gambol at the diminishing or will you
push me to the vanishing? It's simply not polite.
Two points of no return masquerade
where matter is no sleight of hand.

Re: your point. "Stay." You
make a such good One.

Point of fact: This could be the halfway or the end.
Life: Version 1 point — What do I want? Do we have enough to win?
      At sum
I find true dimension zero.

Head still, tail extended, you mark the game.
What exactly is —   Gasoline to the frustration I raise
white flag to the ballerina box in full flight.
en pointe.
Pivot to points north.

Pen and parchment: a stationary pith. Relative minima.
—   blank.
Let's leave it on the counter. Point of fact:

Camus was right.
Men must live and create.
Camus was wrong.
Live to the point of tears.

No.   More

                    to that.

DAVID KOEHN

Short Circuit

No Facebook for the magpie on the barbed wire,
The never open white-paneled door of the local market.

Trying to connect. Limited bandwidth. Connection
Failed. The steeple's antenna, the only cell service

Until Cayuchos. My iPhone held high. Still no bars
Available but Budweiser on display for $22.00 a case.

Apparently, someone's God has got a good connection.
The conversation would be quick, I'd be like, "What's

Up?" Then complain about the coverage. After he
Told me what thought I needed to know, because he'd

Know what that was, I'd pop a breath mint. Even though
That would never cover the stink. I'd add, "Tell mom hi."

A brown-eyed young man in a Cheap Trick t-shirt steps by
"You could not get me to drink that shit if you paid me."

RICHARD O'BRIEN

The Wrong Places

When they say dark matter I don't know
what that means; no more than, say, the
theoretical physicist who knows that anger
& sadness are unyielding powers that fit no
speculative model of composition, powers
that cannot be destroyed. What if the thing
that holds it all together — the dark energy
that makes up more than sixty percent of the
known universe — is equal parts desolation
& despair? Maybe the theoretical physicists
are looking in the wrong places for answers;
perhaps the poets, too.

CLAUDIA RODRIGUEZ

Break Me a Sunrise in a Cup

Break me a sunrise
in a cup, mix its rawness
with my coffee. Warms it up!
Perfect protein punch, poking
my innards, fire ants in my belly.
Pushes me outwards —
unzip my skin and step out of myself.
Sunrise in a cup makes me strong,
body-builder's mind bending roads ahead.
Makes my smile a Las Vegas glitz,
morning greet bona fide,
got any doorman beat.
Heartbeat scattered
as I crown a new day.

MOBI WARREN

Early Morning Runs that Became Rescues

I.

A young possum hit by car, four dead babies strewn about her
like spokes of a wheel. I lifted the four survivors, bewildered
and squirming. Folded my shirt into a pouch and tucked them in.

2.

A nighthawk with broken wing crouched in speckled grasses. As
I lifted her, dark eyes swallowed me, tiny beak opened to a wide bell.

3.

Heart froze then sped— buck hanging from a spear-tipped fence.
Pierced groin, haunches wedged, thread of breath fading. I roused
neighbors. We heaved him up and over. He bounded, leapt. He lived.

4.

A hiss like castanets stopped me, the false rattle of a bull snake
tangled in garden webbing. Praise the keeled scales that excited
my hands. I cut him free.

Hairball 6

Don't rush
To explore
Most humans
Are immune
To understanding
If you leave
Close the door
To open the
Door, if necessary
Semi-closed
Eyes show
Trust. Balance
Leaping, listen
For anything
Approaching: ear
A wide range
Each ear
Is independent
Ear, ears, ear-
Ing. Salty, bitter
Sour & sweet, the
First three suffer

Note: This poem is an erasure on "The Secret Language of Cats" by Heather Dunphy

Karen L. George

Blindsided

While away in the Blue Ridge Mountains,
I dreamt of Mom, the details fuzzy
but not the unease,
like a sunburn that scolds
every move you make.

Back home, I tell her about hiking
in Shenandoah Forest past a deer lair
under pines, how we swam, soaked
in an outdoor hot tub, spied
squirrels, deer, a skunk,
sipped wine while we eyed
the sky for golden eagles.

I want to describe the fat woodchuck,
palm-size patch of fur missing,
how it rose on hind legs
to beg; but I sense a shift,
and when I ask, she reveals
trouble sleeping, struggles to breathe,
how she told her team she can't finish
the season, though she's bowled
in leagues sixty years.

When she admits some days
she can't stop worrying,
badgers herself out of bed,
it reminds me of when we entered
dense fog — the jolt

of being unmoored,
then relief
of our breakthrough.

I try not to think how it feels
when your life dwindles
to a near blindness
you can't drive through.

Mariela Griffor

Chambers (for U. L.)

"And thou thyself, Calliope."
— Sappho

I.

Place of amber and gold
where he as a shark arises:
Let no bounds keep us in
garments of greed and no fun!
Let these men's thoughts sway free.

II.

I have measured my defeat
a hundred times, at the edge
of his grave but clearly
under your potent flames,
the wall does not crumble.

III.

Behold the red bells
for you will need them,
keep your blå-sippor, they
will crash further
in your leaderless hand.

IV.

The "Lady of the Books" he
did baptize her, working
on the prison of his fields,
stealing infamous mortality
from the Sundial's Bofors.

V.

Bright yellow and blue
star incomparable beyond
limits so exposed like scars.
How many glorious predestined sites
fall each day under your glow?:
"We have taken lives and saved much more."

VI.

Are you really alive
under your dirty skin?
Who commands your battles?
Who kills in your name?
At what time of the day do you
perfect your machines?

VII.

You, treacherous, secret little wisdom
learned at the very Royal Institute of Technology,
computed profits of low essence,
citadel of swelling fragments,
kakelugn of scattered fathers and sons.

VIII.

Somewhere at some frontiers
your mouth is salivating
with their lives.

IX.

I will wait until
the mountains can talk,
until the ground tells
me where his voice crumbled.
I will drink from his last breath,
O, you inspire, you inspire me
to know your name.

X.

I will connect all the pieces
of his memory in your Cathedrals.
I will speak only with his voice
so you feel the terror, hunted,
populated by mother earth's trembling anger.
I will know all your names and sing them
in a hymn of immortal cries —

XI.

I stand in a dark alley
trying to pour out light
from this hollow carcass.
I litter among a wreath of disaster

leaking shadows wherever I go.
All that remains is the time the sun swallowed.

XII.

I know this Great River should be prudent:
    As all the great rivers it wants to run free
with unconditional allies and faithful followers:
the shark will not swallow all the waters or men.
    I will wait whetting my actions from between
        my index finger and my thumb.

RACHEL KUBIE

how to keep a country

sing in buses up the mountain side
from the backs of trucks unload the folding chairs
fill up the public squares and in the breeze
outside the courthouse test the mics
test the bullhorns write your jokes and poems
on the poster board file over the bridges
and under the bridges and along the way
while the person next to you is listening
the two of you are house and senate
magnanimous in the sunshine

DENISE RODRIGUEZ

My Father's Farm: Tierra Madre

for my father, Jaime Bustos

Each sprouting surface reveals flesh
of the earth, molded from the soil like clay.
The ground is for more
than burying bones. Every bloom from the land,
a release of breath from deep inside your lungs.

You pull each brilliant shape from the dirt,
hold them in your hands, compare skins
marked with scars from growing,
dazed by how they seem to breathe
in your palms.

M. E. SILVERMAN

The Last Jew and the Wall

Yellow-white like mid-day sun,
the stacked square pavers
still stand, a half-built house
or half-fallen.

Many stones are cracked,
open chunks or thin spread webs,
nested with folded papers
or patches of green weeds.

Every day except Saturday,
the old man appears,
sits hunched, back pressed
to the wall, familiar friends

sharing a space, sharing secrets.
He grips carefully written prayer
rolled like a cigarette,
chants in a forgotten language.

Wearing a small cap
and his grandfather's shawl,
he forgets the meaning of it
but keeps the tradition.

The horizon hurts with white light.
A few students stop with change.
Tourists tap their digital guidebooks,
read about Kotel and Herod,

the bulldozed Moroccan Quarter.
A small footnote mentions the old man,
not by name, just his song,
the echo of a million shooting stars.

SCOTT WHITAKER

Love in Reverse

Because I unfound you there is no reason to stay
and count the lashes horse tails make,
or carry beanpoles and buckets of bluebells
across yardways. They are matters for feet who are true.
There is no reason to stay. Have not your wants
grown up with wants of their own? The meddling
an old horse can manage when fences have fallen down
in rain and wind. Because I unfound you
you must go. You must walk for a while in your own music,
which is to say I cannot tune or conduct.
The lifting up of the neck of the guitar is your own.
Because I unfound you there is no reason to stay.
The skeleton of the buck at the end of our lane
has grown up with flowers, weeds cover bone.
You cannot stay. The hound at the end of his chain
has worn away the grass. Nothing grows and your pockets
have seeds, Chinese coins, wet cigarettes and matches.
When I found you the earth had given you up by the river.
The language for breaking had been written for you.
Your lonely tongue, pretty as salmon cake,
belonged to lovely loops because silence was something for the weak
and dying. You must leave and unfind your way here.
Take your strange verbs and the old tin boxes to rattle
when the wind doesn't blow. There is no reason for you to stay.

Janelle Adsit

A Keystroke Made

ampersand for true, squiggly for thought
without language
the semiotics of blood and pulse

at sign for god, pilcrow for find
asterisk to chart the posture that has me in a truce

a caret to say we might have been
in some kind of emergency

parentheses for the river
hastening to take us
parentheses to keep us
playing in that river

pound sign to follow
the uncontained river that filled her
now uncontained body

ellipsis to mark the where of the stream

after the colon I will want to get to the river
brackets for yearn
a tilde for beautiful valley
space bar for the ash that we never got around
to spreading

at sign for the rarefied gesture
of planting her in land

plus sign for the silent sounding of alone

Stevie Edwards

Effort at Quiet

after Muriel Rukeyser

Dark orbs glide before my eyes
worse when tired
but never gone. I am never alone
with doors closed,
always something sniveling
watching me undress in sweat air.
When I say something
I mean him.
I'd rip myself out of this skin
and throw it to him like a rawhide toy
if I could find a way.
What am I
now? Not less than body,
I can't be for I have wept
my lungs sore.
I can feel myself feeling
noise of the news
as it twitters in the automated sky.
God of thunder, God of night,
let the stars say no
horoscopes. It is the year of the mute
swan. It is the year we drown
our tongues in ocean and let
salt sting all our sores.
It is the year of not asking
the moon, the grass, the wrench,
the candlestick, or heaven
questions about death.

SINA EVANS

fan the fire

threaded through with light and October
  I'm feeling kind-of-Kate today, she blurbs
thin the friction, thin the flame
  I spat blue at the fire as it burned
——the gloss the glass of water, a spark
  cornflower, glacier, pail, seafaring and bottle
chorus, hives, harmony, bullet
  none enough, slicker through and through
the buzz of beasts unburdened
  enough, enough enough blue.

ANITA FELICELLI

Migration

Pelicans chase salt
to our estuary, drawn
by salt heliotrope creeping
over sodden banks,
wild fennel — an inferno

of golden hills, the death-smell
of trash rot, sulfurous algae
under water, in decay.
I chase pelicans on foot,
my sneakers rubbing away webbed
runes in silt. I chase the myth-
making of their ungainly calls,
a susurrus past red thickets —
island rookery, hot dazzle.

When you scent salt,
no perfume emerges, yet somehow
when you smell it rising from the wet
shore line, surging like a revenant
through ice plants and sunlight,
a moment of recognition —
so *this* is salt,
these are pelicans
in their infinite return.

LUCIA GALLOWAY

Turquoise

Traded at Turkish bazaars to merchants en route
across the continent, the sky-blue gem from Persia rose
to prominence in Europe, where if legend tells us true,
it took its name, *turquois*, from the site
where sandaled traders dug in dusty toes.
Does this make turquoise ours?
I like believing that the Anasazi, skilled at quoits,
eager in the turquoise trade, also prospered in that quest,
thriving in our canyons until adversity came to rout
them. Quiet hues of sky and water filled a seam, suture
in the rock of a deeper tier. From this ground the osier
drew its drink. Ancient rites
paid homage to gods of what seemed sure,
that water would run and the sun would rise.

CHARLOTTE MATTHEWS
We Meet at the Ritz

Not a place I usually find myself
but I said okay because he suggested it,
and when I googled him there was a
bird's eye view of a mansion in Darien
a flawless photo of his wife and three kids.

Mostly I wanted to see him because
he knew my mother and I held hope
he'd remember her eyes or the way she folded her napkin
squarely in her lap all the while making an observation
so appalling and accurate it made you freeze.

It's suddenly fall, and I'm lost in our nation's capital
on my way to have a beer with my first ever boyfriend.
I ask strangers where the Ritz is, run one block, walk
the next, feel like a chicken with my head cut off.
And guess what? I was thinking I'd look all easy breezy

when the doorman put his gloved hand on the polished knob,
pointed me to the bar. I was thinking I could do this, turn back
time for an hour. But I forgot that when our science teacher taught
us the solar system I knew he was actually warning us about
ourselves, all that matter spinning in and collapsing on itself.

PETER VANDERBERG

One One-Thousand

The sacred demands our attention

with lightning & sudden deluge. Wordless
questions are answered by a pillar of broken sky
& we have left ordinary time.

A thunderstorm soaks everything in revelation.
Young & afraid, my father told me that each second
before thunder equals our distance from lightning.
After each flash, I count. I want my god

to reveal sure signs, but also to keep his distance:
five miles or more. No one likes a close-talker.
Every broadleaf & pine exhales His breath.
The morning's cardinals & cicadas

have silenced. Rain abates & the chorus
resounds in the wake of passing epiphany.

SCOTT WEAVER

And I, Agnolo

*"And I, Agnolo di Turi, called The Fat, buried my five children with my own hands,
and so did many others likewise."*

— Chronicle of Siena, during the Black Death

Now I cannot stop thinking of him, fat drops of sweat dripping
from the tip of a nose as bulbous as a garlic clove
into the fresh-turned dirt at his feet, how each salty drop
disappeared into the earth until this long-avoided labor
had made mud of the ground outside his city.

It began when I handed our four-month-old to the man
who'd introduced himself as Mike that morning
outside the Cold War-themed bar where we sat eating
our haggard new-parent brunch.
No one to bury his sons, imagine the sight
he must have made to burghers peering out
from shuttered houses — faith, good works replaced
by castled fear of poisoned wells, the ceaseless wrath
of God or stars but finally death, watching the small figure
of The Fat in evening light throwing dirt.
Only when Mike staggered backward toward Sixth Street
under the new weight of our daughter did I see he'd been drinking
well before the sun had risen. Another ten seconds and it had passed,
daughter safe on my knee, an unfamiliar strain of guilt
sweeping across my chest like pestilence come
to some Rhône village and its now-tested faith.

As the Black Death took Avignon, the Pope's physician wrote
A father did not visit his son, nor the son his father. Charity was dead.
Forgive me. When I passed my child to Mike that morning
I thought I saw in him a longing I might briefly ease.
Now all I see is night's black where Agnolo must be digging

surrounded by doors locked not so tight as to block the burning
lights at his back, each one reminding him he is worse than alone.

H. V. CRAMOND

Oh God, It's Happening

for food poisoning

last grasp at control
cauterized in all directions
purge strength purge plans

there is only
this porcelain moment
of eyes-closed certainty:

fuck you Trader Joe's
and the excessive packaging
you rode in on

MELISSA CUNDIEFF-PEXA

Voice As Beginning, As End

Chair'd in the adamant of Time.
— Walt Whitman

When my daughter says she wants her infancy back.
I say I would go back too, when I could still hold her,
when I could speak saturnine and aloud, like this,
"Someday I will vanish inside you. You will
think of me like a stitch dissolved." And then, also,
my tired nonsense, "You're a bird. You're a bird."
Always, my daughter wouldn't answer but stare
with her wet, infant eyes like teacups on a burning
blanket. I would continue, sometimes, like this,
"There's a cliff leaving its height in my heart ..."
Now in the future where my daughter, so close to grown,
says, "I want to be yours again, to root,
to nurse," I realize it is she who has disappeared
inside me. That first version of herself, all synapse
before word, tears to show her hunger, no question yet,
no answer. I speak in my way, "We have left each other
for each other. The body wishes. Is a wish."

CHRISTINE GOSNAY

California Spleen

In their 6 body chamber orchard, my grandfather's trees gave
fruit too quickly to the earth, they nourished the ground. Soft
through my toes, I starved on them,
maturing, I learned the names and believed
I had the upper hand. They couldn't speak back,
Ashmead's Kernel, Bartlett, paper mulberry.

I watch a grown man lean against nothing, his silhouette reclined
against negative space, married to its
endless capabilities.
Either a parlor trick or the center of a slow fall.
Has any clung as tightly to his fears as a panicle
to its drupe, bone white like the rowan's, blood pink

the Schinus molle's? To be an animal takes the courage of
resignation, the soul to own a spleen, never known for its
purpose until it meets with harm, for its silent lurk of love,
dutiful organ, quiet clump against the restive world.
If someone should remove me piece by piece
he will find the seeds, at least, of fruit, if not the bullying flesh.

LAUREL KALLEN

Who is Ready?

for the strike and puncture,
for drainage of the ghee

of life, till bodies too
scathed and dry won't answer,

a scratch and whisper is
all we are splotches, sprawled

shadows on the floors, our
rooms exhaust themselves to

the tick of the clock more
positive than our laugh,

the parched home crumbles — a
powder of no matter,

in the beginning, I
heard smile, saw understand

eyes like oceans' swirl blue
green, grey and deepen, the

will more willful waxes
thickest love wants membranes.

JEN KINDBOM

A Flock of Haiku is Called a Train

Clearly, the fact that
you're taking a photograph
makes you immune to

imminent danger
inherent to standing on
frequented railroad

tracks. Go ahead, set
your first born right there on the
warm rail. I'll forget

when we were all kids
taking coins across the field
waiting out a train,

balancing them on rails
still hot from a mile of freight —
waiting for a flat

penny, monument
smeared into segments on a
hot copper oval,

landing in the rocks
or flung into the high grass
where we played softball —

all of our parents
chilling in the shade of trees
grilling ears of corn

(showing us how to
wait until it's pretty safe
and balance pennies).

Can't you hear it from
where you're standing? Don't you think
you should maybe move?

I guess it's romance
to forget what could kill you
before you see it

   — or nostalgia, or
parallels and vanishing
points: a perfect shot.

Laurin Becker Macios

I Am Telling You This Story Because

I am an empty glass jar turning yellow in the sun.
The dried flowers inside me are heavier than a child.
I am a day seven years ago sung full of life by an Irish
lyric, a Roman stone pillar, a cup full of wine. I am
drugged on a nice doctor's table and she opens her
beautiful whale mouth to tell me it will all soon be over,
only her mouth is turning silver and sounds like an engine,
her gloved hands are the noon sea spreading and I
am an ice cap, you are a turtledove, I am sleeping.

KARA PENN

What We Learn from Crows

Everything outlandishly green
for mid-October, leaves loath
to change. Epic sky cloudless, crisp.

New Mexico scrub shifts to Colorado
plain and pine, scarred peak and hill.
Late sun slants. Loudmouth crows hurtle

against relentless gusts in muted discipline.
They turn back from the crack-opened vista
beckoning its blues and unexplored,

prepare for what's promised —
ruthless ice and glass-cold. They
prepare for what's not, blistering up

late spring's hot, as smoke in stone's
lichen, spreading wide and over
into ravenous and gaping inferno, gulping

trees, the nests they hold. Each season,
what to do but hover, speechless?

CHARLES A. SWANSON

Testimony of the House

Age has taught me change. I was so young,
despite three grandparents passing, I assumed
that life goes on. No change in any room,
where things were made, white oak chair seats, turned rungs
and curtain rods, dove-tailed corners, the wood tongued
or notched. Through thread or yarn, flowers bloomed
in fingerwork. Without even a loom
imagination took shape, hand-sewn, hand-sung.
So little had changed, I could not arrive
at what had. Some of this hand-work was Grandpa's,
who was already gone. He sawed the soapstone
for the fireplace, laid the rocks. He rived
the wood for wall and roof. My sense was flawed,
but endurance spoke in things, things of home.

KELLEEN ZUBICK

From the Shore

Father rows the oars as if wind
were never returning. Gulls have broken
morning silence on the water
where he pushes forward and heaves
back, grooved as pure mechanism,
as if the skiff were chasing mirage
toward the center of Lake Washington.

What does he want beyond
the reach of us? Dave Brubeck
back on the radio of the Studebaker
on open road through Idaho;
a last round of Schlitz with Jim May
before Alzheimer's? How little
we know of his 48 working years,

travel and glass-fronted meetings
above foreign cities that made him
stranger to the rest of us who've taken
or kept his name. His drive always
unknowable but sure — a past of skipped
anniversaries and single-handed
sailing in the North and Norwegian Seas.

Not us. He's come to depend on trial, testing
his persisted body, impulsively fighting
like the herons flying low, too far
from shore. He's still strong through water,
raising small caps with his passage.
It's a state of clean element; he's here
to give something his all in one last way.

PAUL BROOKE

A Smack of Jellies

written after visiting the Shedd Aquarium, Chicago, Illinois

As a child, one rubbed his arm, bumping its thin trail of tendrils.
Welts bubbling. His mother knew, held him out of the ocean for years.

And then he surfed, swam, jet skied, snorkeled, skim boarded:
his mother frantic on shore, waiting for a pronouncement or a body.

Stung by a smack of jellyfish, his hands became algaed stones;
he drifted in the pink current like a scarf until plucked

By a kayaker, who somehow jumpstarted his heart. Underwater,
he hated everything, harbored ill will, hurled insults at his mother.

Now, he stands in front of a swarm, pulsating against bright blue,
ancient, strung by a multiplicity of toxic cells, stinging barbs.

He is aware of no one. An hour passes and he drifts with them,
upsurging in rhythmic beauty. Children freewheeling into him.

Swarms of people floating by like colorful rafts. He savors the feeling,
the sensation of flying, of simple equations built of water, built of now.

Lisa J. Cihlar

You Just Need a Good Cry and You Will Feel Better

The whoosh when the furnace comes on for the first time in fall after frost has settled on the horse pasture twice. Smell of hot dust, then a sneeze. I hate cold November rains bringing down the last leaves. The orrery that is this world seems to be missing a tooth on one cog and is stuck on shortest days and longest nights. Long nights that used to be full of love are now just tired and grumpy. The heater I turn on to warm my legs has a tinny rattle. It makes my fillings sting. There are some who think that mercury in my teeth is the cause of all of my problems. Mercury is small and close to the sun. It runs hot and cold. The sun has been absent for eight days now. There is no proof that it will ever return.

LISA FAY COUTLEY

Never, & One-Thousand Years Ago

Maybe even then, maybe especially then,
shamans knew the way, in the future, we'd be

able to look through glass into our own pores
& see stars, dust, the skin as terrain like any

other forcing forward through complete dark.

The way only years later, & now, you know
you never stood to leave that room, never rested

your plastic fork on its Styrofoam dish, still stuck
through the halved planet of a Brussels sprout,

never entered that blinding light & warm March

through doors parting before you without needing
touch. Never can you go back & hold your own

small hand holding hers heavy in a colorless bed
where every tethered star burns bright & dying

in her boundless mouth, open as a bird's, a mother's

coaxing peas to her child. Never will you know
his name, the man reeling from her a clear, plastic

tube ribbed like sand, ribs of cloud, ribs catching
both corners of her mouth. Infinite. Wound

with tinder ahead. Wound with fire behind.

PHYLLIS HOGE

Like Trees

James Rosen's "Madonna and Child After Cimabue"

On a rectilinear base of peach-colored marble
Mary, gowned in a honey-colored stole,
and centered under the weight of December sun,
dissolves beneath her halo
among attendant angels hovering by
and Cousin John.

Becoming ethereal she is at peace. Easy.
She is like any other woman
slowly growing accustomed to her baby
and to motherhood, all it requires,
her marvelous body passive to what happens,
bearing the gift. It's just how it is.
She'll do whatever is needed.
Comfort. Milk. Sleep. Bath. Laundry.

She is as casual and unconscious as trees
when glistening leaves, having been storm-blown
or stilled amid sheer midsummer heat,
undergo their slow transfiguration.

Today, winter sunlight spins down in shafts
broken by leaves that shiver into gold, wrinkle,
and drift down to the ground
ignorant of their glory.

She glows like trees.
The afternoon sun feels good to her.

JOAN NAVIYUK KANE

Under Another Winter

Immured aside a drift of skimmed blue clay
near crests occur immense, mounting, a thaw
rolling in reverse, relapsed over, rending

to an ebb less vague than vanished —
his hood diminished to a bud, bole or flaw
below the aniline rise of chalk clouds to sky

as she would sift her grief for him, insisting
his wake a sulcus one could not withdraw,
wheel back, fault or lapse again, rendered.

To her wishes I would gather fuel, manage
its ash, split the damp pulp from bark, haul
spent trunks jettisoned by marine gray mass.

The other camps from which she was banished
were filled with men whose poles caught the raw
wind to dry the skins of their torn burdens.

Her wrist, rift of ornaments & gifts, a myth.
Her past a brawl: it leaves one pinned, hauled
against the inside of the horizon's bleached skull,
his songs bloat & bruise with flood & breakers all.

ERIKA LUTZNER

My mouth is made of bird bones

framed shrines contain the miniature bits
of leftover scraps of flesh and skeleton.
I try scaffolding myself with paper mâché, but
I keep disintegrating. I am in a closet in the back
of a truck on the highway between Arizona and Utah.
I meant to get off in Nevada, but limbs kept
falling from the sky. There's a window in the middle of
Kentucky; if I can make it that far.

MICHAEL J PAGÁN

If that sun doesn't get over the hill, she's late

Magic gray ribbon of
men; I believed that wind.

Silent, dignified, that father's
way: big flaps over pockets
hiding hills made of boulders
of giants of children of giants
growing tired of play —
it killed them, but
there were plenty more wings
collapsed — they'd been shot off.

And feet can be a trifle, then.
Little red lines counting just
how fast they'd gone, how far
they'd fallen.

The boy knew change.
Never would the boy forget
that day when they'd invented
a device of mirrors: Her hair
an anemic brown. To a man,
a woman's tears are a minute
animal, nearly or quite invisible
to the naked eye.

Her, with nothing
else to wipe. Each bit
of cloth needed to cover
bare legs, so she slid
off the boulder, then asked:

"What is it that makes
your earthquakes?"

Far off, they had been blue.
Now, they lay in tumbles
like fog-laden plants
on the sides of roads.

You wanted wings. It was new
to breathe. The fog had blurred
their falconry; hair-filling moisture
trickling down his forehead
and into his eyes, believing
the sun with its overcoat big
with collars and the horn-rimmed
glasses of an oculist sweeping
crumbs from a table.

Attitude, that of a shiny
new gold watch, because to a man
clothing is a part of man's dignity;
a symbol of their rise.

Therefore, the boy knew
chains when screaming: "She's
trying to get away! Oh father,
step on her!"

"Damn fool!" he answered back.

And sure enough, the clouds
died and the boy left with nothing
but his respects for a beautiful
piece of machinery, painting
a sign reading "Free Air."

BILL PRINDLE

The Following Day

Yesterday a great pileated alighted in the black walnut tree,
Inclined his sovereign crested head, flew off toward the river.
The candidates caravan came through, last governor, next
Governor, Congressman's daughter, all hope and urgency.

Today the turkey buzzards wheel in the northerly wind,
Slow to the point of insolence, the holdout maples are lit
From within. No power comes near, no eye meets mine,
I lift the well cover and holler down for the boy I forgot.

A. M. THOMPSON

March Thaw

Scour out the dark
bits clinging
to the wound.

Rush down
my sluicing earth
like glacier melt.

Rinse out the grief
and grudges,

deep sand
craving
at the core.

Clear waterlight
of Sky: wash free

and as you do
let mercy leave me

nourished as you pass.

Carolee Bennett

How to construct a diorama

Hold out your arms as if practicing the waltz alone at home.
That's the frame, stiff cardboard, that demonstrates understanding
of all you have read, which is also replica of all the places,
loosely embraced, you have lived. Animals will come and go.
And parents. Do not glue those down. Search drawers for trinkets
that may be significant. However, consider all objects even
slightly admissible. Details like: the portraits on the wall and
slippers at the bedside, lip smudges on the rim of a glass of red wine,
coffee grounds in a paper filter timed to drip in the morning
between shower and commute. The written report — on blue-lined
composition paper, your name, homeroom and date at the top and
in pencil — reveals a tenth of what you know. (Do not be teacher's pet.
Do not be the example of an "A" project.) Show also the man
who stands at the door, flowers behind his back. Or a knife.
(Sometimes there is a threat.) And an artificial tree stuffed in a closet.
A kitchen table with popsicle birdhouse in progress. A child
who runs in because she's seen a snake. On the TV, warnings:
another hurricane. And upstairs, a tree already against the corner
of the house where the baby sleeps in his crib. Except that night
he goes to bed with his mother. The roof remains in disrepair,
homage to what may have saved him. It snows inside now,
and that is part of the oral report when you'll wish there were
a way to make small curtains mimic what real curtains do
when the wind blows and that everyone may hear the music
you hear from up on this stage, the pit band's horn popping up
to catch the off-beats: the joy! the joy! the joy! the joy? Until:
a classmate points, asks, *What is that* when the teacher insists
there must be questions. *Me*, you answer. In the tree I climb.
In the garden I turn over. In the corner I hide. And there I sit

on the edge of —————— *Well, what* the teacher presses,
as if possibilities were real curtains. The only wrong answer:
hospital bed. They came for it. It is no longer there.

KATE FADICK

Canticle with Tight-Fitting Lids

after Aimee Nezhukumatathil

Blessed be the lover who finishes laundry,
brings me this cold day's first coffee.

Blessed be the potter who shapes the cup,
her hands that find wolves in clay.

Blessed be raccoons leaving calligraphy
in overnight snow and tight-lidded bins

the city provides. Blessed be the mourning
dove foraging alone among seeds below

the feeder, three cardinals watching from
the muted trumpet vine. Blessed be any

friend who cannot remember how to cipher
a tip, no longer drives, yet still loves vintage

Buicks and that one last ride with the top down.

Anthony Frame

Christmas Poem

The part I'm most interested in is the part
where he's also 100% human, the part where
he's a budding baby reaching for his mother's milk,
where he sees the world around him but isn't
sure how big it is. I imagine him learning to talk,
his tongue testing its limits, his mind tasting
each syllable as they stretch through his throat.
And that first wobbly step, did he smile, did he
shine with pride like the clouds in all those paintings?
I forget, sometimes, that he was a boy, chasing snakes
or digging holes in the sand, playing desert games
with the other desert boys. I like him that way,
human, flesh and bone and muscle, a scraped knee,
a wondering eye as it watches the birds soaring through
the sky. I know there's more to him than me, but even
if he's all you say, I'm not sure that's the best part.
The best part is the idea that god could have a little bit
of me in him, that even god's voice, once in a while,
might crack in the middle of a song. I like that like
I like the man looking up, looking beyond the clouds,
beyond even the stars. I can believe in the man who
looked at the sky and, like me, sighed with longing.

YVETTE FROCK GOTTSHALL

Karen's Poem

Karen's poem was about a pine cone
and layers and layers of releasing.

We went around our workshop
circle giving comments and I said

why not say, "I am a pine cone?" to
which everyone laughed and said

"you can't write 'I am a pine cone'
in a poem." I thought poetry was/is

about the can and not the can't;
about the things we can utter

and not about keeping silent. I,
for example, am driftwood.

I've been tumbled and moved
across many bodies of turbulent

frothing waters. Water teeming with,
"Yankee go home" and "Why you here?"

I've drifted over the Sea of Marmara;
the Atlantic where it's poured through

that place where the East China Sea
meets the Philippine Sea. I've been

tumbled clean of accents, although I pick
these up easily. I've been washed of all

the identifying features of every culture
I've invested in order to claim an identity,

a with-ness, a belonging. My sense of time
relations, for example; must I arrive exactly

on time, like the brat I've been trained to be
or a little late, or just a few minutes early —

what is acceptable to my host?
My sense of spatial relations, for another:

Do I stand a foot apart or close
enough to smell the breath? What

about shoes? Worn in the house, or not permitted?
What about hands? May I use either or only

the right? Is it "you guys" or is it "y'all"?
So being driftwood, I see no reason why

Karen can't be a pine cone.

Fascination with Sky

nights

fighting　　　　　　*order of thought*

Far back in the mine,
only clink of pick against endless wall
　　　　　of　　　　　　*idea of being*

lost

　　　　what became soot
　　when you emerged to daylight.
　　　losing　　　　　　　*hold*

　　　　　　　　　　under

　　weight of　　*space*

Sometimes you saw stars
　　in the glare of headlamp,
　　　　　could pick out constellations,

but sometimes you were afraid
　　　you'd keep on hammering
　　　　　just to get a glimpse of sky

until it all fell down on you,
　　　what could be diamond
　　　　　had you not traveled a sea
　　　　　　to be here.

Note: The text in italics is from a 1913 first edition of Zane Grey's Desert Gold.
*At 3 AM, 1/23/1907, twenty-four "lives went out," the entire shift, reported as all
foreigners, at Primero Mine owned by CF&I. Had the explosion occurred during the
day over a hundred would have been entombed. Final count: nineteen Hungarians, four
Italians, and one Welsh, details hard to obtain at the company store.*

Runoff

These slick-barked trees are nothing
like me, they lack
softness to the touch,
easy unpeeling.

Heaven knows which direction their moss points.

Where I am from it is always north.
But I have been assigning meaning
to the world so long
I have forgotten how to count

rootlessness a blessing.

There is a reason the birds hop.
I do not know what it is.
Maybe their bird joints stiffen
when they refrain from flight,

heeding the planet's pull for now.

One-third of a bird's legs are invisible, hidden
in the body, the other two fold back
and in, aerodynamic, unlike the wasp,
all leg and sharp and dangle

who will not bleed if his wings are plucked.

Nature does not make noise, only sounds.
You are the quiet one. You are
the one who renames water
when it touches earth, unchanged.

Coyote

Night was quietest in deep cold. Cold redder than a fire
leaps a dormant mind. Mandatory skirting of the known
perimeters: know means known. Densest blue possibly
nicked with pulsing. Bodies trapped and still singing. If
astral is a flower.

Set traps have a scentless way of being. Constant field
the tawny nature of our mange. Forced to rest and heal
when distance is the only cure.

On the hunt exhilaration is the clean appetite. We leave
easy prey for lesser wiles. Cities sniff around too near
our middens. In the earth are stones hardly inscribed.

Our riches are in rinds and woodpiles. Discards
the truth of treasure. Lean and boned to shine.

KUSHAL PODDAR

Laughter for My Neighbors, Cry for the Shadows

Neighbors are bothered by loud laughter
but not by loud weeping.
— Ben Lerner

Five thirty in the evening. Winter.
The real shadows return home. Others
yawn and begin following us around.

If I stand below this new streetlight
four will sniff my ankles. And one, the fifth,
will roll out its skin so I can see

its inside, made of light, made of night,
made of translucence. I feed them
my laughter to irk our neighbors who

wish I would cry, not from pleasure.
I cannot blame them. How else would they
muffle their own dirge? Go my shadows.

Wake up the home of night. Wake up your
real fathers. The sun will rise sooner than
you imagine.

JULIANZA SHAVIN

Who Do Not Speak Today

The days run away like wild horses over the hills ...
— Charles Bukowski

At the water's edge
all the horses you can't make drink,
pondering long profiles
in feathers of sand.

I'm out doing things I dislike, he says.
I say, *I'm in all day, as is the dog
who's brought no news*

*no twigs in tail
no thistles in coat
no mischased cat
no dollops of deer*

Line of sound, bird like a cloud? he offers.
No, I must concoct my own cocaine.

Won't say simply what he sees —
my need hundreds the herd
which slumps to the sea
close-mouthed and drowned.

The dog's legs do not twitch.
Semi-invalid these many years
I accede to thirst. Blind
I harness to dry blind dreams.

KATHARINE WHITCOMB

The Bird

Outside the door of my rented cottage
lay a dead bird. As I heaved my book bag onto a chair he was there,
close to the wall, out of the sightline of the room.

His body was so large the look of him
paralyzed me, orange, handsome orange, black with a bright beak.
A foot and leg curled onto the cement, long

feathers like a cape. Formal. Fluid
in a wet pool under his beak. The day blue at noon. Time stops,
you know, with death. I could not do anything

without first attending to him. I was not
prepared or brave. I found a bag, a big napkin and a glove.
Stood over him, knelt on the rough deck,

said *bird bird bird bird bird*.
I was afraid he was stunned, not moving; that he would try
to fly and was not yet dead. I did not want

to make it worse for him. But
when I leaned in close over his white-ringed eye there was no flicker,
gone. To touch him was not grave, but easy,

light. I have no one
to give me advice on these things. I carried him across the green
lawns to a dumpster. I wished then

more than ever for solitude.
Even the strangers inhabiting their quiet cottages were terrible.
If you sit still, they say, everything finds you.

Acknowledgments

The following poems appeared previously in these publications:

"Hawks in Harvard Square" by Lisa DeSiro, in *Commonthought Magazine.*

"how to keep a country" by Rachel Kubie, in *Mudlark Flash.*

"Shades of White" by Diana Khoi Nguyen, in *Phoebe.*

Contributors Notes

Janelle Adsit's poetry, book reviews, and essays have appeared in *Confrontation, Caketrain, Mid-American Review, ForeWord,* and *Colorado Review.* She teaches writing at the San Francisco Art Institute.

Carolee Bennett is an artist and poet who lives in Albany, New York, with her three sons. Her poetry has been published in a number of print and online journals, and she is pursuing an MFA in poetry through Ashland University in Ohio.

Justin Boening is the author of *Self-Portrait as Missing Person,* winner of a Poetry Society of America's National Chapbook Fellowship. Currently he is an associate editor for *Poetry Northwest* and lives in Lewisburg, Pennsylvania, where he is a Stadler Fellow in Poetry at Bucknell University.

Paul Brooke has published two previous books of poetry and photographs, *Light and Matter* and *Meditations on Egrets* (both Campbell & Lewis, 2008 and 2010), and his newest book, *Sirens and Seriemas: Photographs and Poems of the Amazon and Pantanal,* will be published in 2014 by Brambleby Books of London, England. He is a professor of English at Grand View University in Des Moines, Iowa.

Serena Chopra is a PhD candidate in creative writing at the University of Denver. She is the author of *Penumbra* (Flying Guillotine Press, 2011) and *This Human* (Coconut Books, 2013). She lives and works in Denver where she is also a dancer, visual artist, and member of a poets' theater, GASP.

Katy Chrisler lives in Texas where she works at The Contemporary Austin, a community museum. She received her MFA from the Iowa Writers' Workshop and was a recent participant in the Land Arts of the American West traveling residency program. Her poems have appeared in *Tin House, Hayden's Ferry Review,* and *Octopus Magazine.*

Lisa J. Cihlar is the author of two chapbooks, *The Insomniac's House* (Dancing Girl Press) and *This Is How She Fails* (Crisis Chronicles Press). Her chapbook *When I Pick Up My Wings from the Dry Cleaner* won the Blue Light Press chapbook contest and was published in 2014.

Alison Cimino lives and volunteers at a meditation retreat center located in the Shenandoah Valley. She also facilitates poetry workshops for teachers and students and teaches a poetry course for educators through Lesley University.

Flower Conroy's first chapbook, *Escape to Nowhere* (Rain Mountain Press), was first runner-up in the Ronald Wardall Poetry Prize. Her second chapbook, *Controlled Burn* (Seven Kitchens Press, forthcoming), was first-runner up in the Robin Becker Poetry Contest. She earned her MFA from Fairleigh Dickinson University.

Lisa Fay Coutley's poetry has been awarded a fellowship from the National Endowment for the Arts, scholarships from the Bread Loaf and Sewanee writers' conferences, and an Academy of American Poets Levis Prize, and have been selected for *Best New Poets* and *Best of the Net*. Her chapbook *In the Carnival of Breathing* won the Black River Chapbook Competition.

Jill Crammond teaches college writing and also children's art and drama classes. Her work has been nominated for a Pushcart Prize and has appeared or is forthcoming in *B: An Anthology of Barbie Poems* (Kind of a Hurricane Press), *burntdistrict*, the e-book anthology of women poets *Fire on Her Tongue* (Two Sylvias Press), and elsewhere.

H. V. Cramond is the poetry editor and a cofounder of *Requited Journal for Innovative Art* and a writing instructor at Loyola University Chicago. She holds an MFA in Writing from the School of the Art Institute of Chicago and has received grants from the Illinois Arts Council and the City of Chicago's Community Arts Assistance Program.

Melissa Cundieff-Pexa's poems have appeared in *Mid-American Review*, *The Collagist*, *Diagram*, and elsewhere. Her manuscript *Your Hindenburg Voice* was a semifinalist for several book prizes as well as a finalist for the Washington Prize. She is currently living with her family in Ithaca, New York, and her chapbook *Futures with Your Ghost* is forthcoming from Finishing Line Press.

Christine Starr Davis holds an MFA from the Vermont College of Fine Arts and was nominated for *Best New Poets 2009* and a 2010 Pushcart Prize. Her work has appeared in *Cider Press Review*, *Confrontation*, *Eclipse*, *Nimrod*, *Permafrost*, *Soundings East*, *Spoon River Poetry Review*, *Studio One*, *Whiskey Island*, and others. She recently won the 2014 Great Plains Emerging Writer Prize.

Holly Day lives in Minneapolis, Minnesota, where she teaches writing classes at The Loft Literary Center. Her poetry has recently appeared in *The Tampa Review*, *The Comstock Review*, and the *Saint Paul Almanac*, and she is the 2011 recipient of the Sam Ragan Poetry Prize from Barton College.

Kate DeBolt teaches eighth graders with special needs in the South Bronx. She is currently in the process of completing her MA in Education at Hunter College and her MFA in Poetry at Sarah Lawrence College. She looks forward to being overeducated and spending her evenings on poems again.

Risa Denenberg is an aging hippie poet who lives in Sequim, Washington, and earns her keep as a nurse practitioner. Her publications include *what we owe each other* (The Lives You Touch Publications, 2013), *Mean Distance from the Sun* (Aldrich Press, 2013), *and blinded by clouds* (Hyacinth Girls Press, 2014).

Lisa DeSiro's poems have appeared in *Mezzo Cammin*, *Sixfold*, and *Poetpourri* (now *The Comstock Review*), and have been used as texts for acclaimed musical compositions. Along with her MFA in creative writing from Lesley University, she has degrees in music and is an accomplished pianist. She lives in Cambridge, Massachusetts.

T. M. De Vos is author of *Cimmeria*, forthcoming from Cervena Barva Press, and she is co-editor-in-chief of Gloom Cupboard. She was awarded a Summer Literary Seminars fellowship for the 2012 session in Vilnius, Lithuania, a Cullman Center fellowship at the New York Public Library, and a Hopwood Award from the University of Michigan.

Donelle Dreese is an associate professor of English at Northern Kentucky University. Her books include *Dragonflies in the Cowburbs* (Anaphora Literary Press), *A Wild Turn* (Finishing Line Press), and *Looking for a Sunday Afternoon* (Pudding House Press). She currently serves as the assistant editor of the *Journal of Kentucky Studies*.

Stevie Edwards is a poet, editor, and educator. Her first book, *Good Grief*, received the Independent Publisher Book Awards Bronze in Poetry and the Devil's Kitchen Reading Award. Her poems have appeared in *Verse Daily*, *Rattle*, *Indiana Review*, *Devil's Lake*, and elsewhere. She is the editor-in-chief of *Muzzle Magazine* and an assistant editor at YesYes Books.

Sina Evans is a poet, maker, and book artist based in Los Angeles. She likes to linger at the intersection where art and language collide. Her latest de-storiéd book is called *Great Days of the Circus* and her first chapbook, *Modern Love*, is forthcoming from dancing girl press.

Kate Fadick comes to her poetry, in part, through her experience as a career community organizer and advocate for social justice in Appalachian communities both rural and urban. Her first chapbook, *Slipstream*, was released by Finishing Line Press in 2013. Recent journal publications include *AEQAI* and *Wind '97*.

Anita Felicelli is the author of a book of poems, *Letters to an Albatross*; a young adult novel, *Sparks Off You*; and a children's book, *Izzy and Poe*. Her writing has appeared in the *New York Times*, *Los Angeles Review of Books*, *The Rumpus*, *Blackbird*, *Babble*, *Rose Red Review*, *Verdict*, and in many other places.

Sally Fisher's poems have appeared in *Poetry East*, *Field*, *The Threepenny Review*, *Margie*, *Mid-American Review*, and many other journals and anthologies. She is a student of improvisation and a stage clown, puppet builder, and sometime performer. She lives in New York City. "Dickinson's Windows" is dedicated to Phyllis Alden.

Rachel Fogarty-Oleson has been supported by the Hampton Arts Management Grant and was the 2010 recipient of the Thomas E. Sanders Scholarship in Creative Writing Award. She serves on the editorial board of Yellow-Jacket Press. Her poems and new media poetic pieces have appeared in *Extract(s)*, *Psychic Meatloaf*, *White Space Poetry Anthology*, *Mobius*, and elsewhere.

Anthony Frame is an exterminator from Toledo, Ohio. He is the author of *A Generation of Insomniacs* (Main Street Rag Press, 2014) and *Paper Guillotines* (Imaginary Friend Press, 2010). His poems have appeared in *Verse Daily*, *Harpur Palate*, *Third Coast*, *The North American Review*, *Versal*, and *diode*, among others.

Naoko Fujimoto was born and raised in Japan. She is currently working on her first collection, *Radio Tower*. She also has a poetry and art project, *Cochlea*, and a poetry and office-environment project, *Killing Sally M. McHill*. Eventually she wants to combine poetry and musical theater. Her creative works are accessible at naokofujimoto.blogspot.com.

Lucia Galloway lives in Southern California, where she earned her MFA in Poetry from Antioch University Los Angeles, and she currently co-hosts Fourth Sundays, a reading series in Claremont. She has authored two poetry collections, *Venus and Other Losses* and the chapbook *Playing Outside*. Her poems have appeared widely in print and online.

Lené Gary lives in Vermont. She holds an MFA from Vermont College of Fine Arts. Her recent publications include pieces in *Please Do Not Remove*, *Up the Staircase*, *Birchsong*, *Poemeleon*, *Limestone*, *Watershed*, *Connotation Press*, *Sage*, and *M Review*. When she is not writing, she can be found paddling her well-worn Mad River canoe.

Karen George, author of *Into the Heartland* (Finishing Line Press, 2011) and *Inner Passage* (Red Bird Chapbooks, 2014), has received grants from Kentucky Foundation for Women and the Kentucky Arts Council. Her work has appeared in *Memoir*, *Louisville Review*, *Still*, *Wind*, *Permafrost*, and *Cortland Review*. She reviews poetry at: http://readwritepoetry.blogspot.com/.

Rebecca Kaiser Gibson's poetry has appeared in *Agni*, *Field*, *Greensboro Review*, *Harvard Review*, *Pleiades*, *Salamander*, *Slate*, *Tupelo Quarterly*, and elsewhere. She has won an Artist Fellowship from the Massachusetts Cultural Council, had residencies at the MacDowell Colony, and received a Fulbright Fellowship to teach in India. She presently teaches poetry at Tufts University.

Christine Gosnay's poetry features in *DIAGRAM*, *Beecher's Magazine*, *[PANK]*, *Squaw Valley Review*, and *THRUSH Poetry Journal*. Founding editor of *The Cossack Review*, she has been a finalist for the Philip Booth Poetry Prize and is an alumna of the Bread Loaf and Squaw Valley writers' conferences. She lives in the Santa Cruz mountains of California.

Yvette Frock Gottshall is a poet and artist who grew up globally and now lives in Vermont. She earned her MFA in Poetry/Translation at Vermont College of Fine Arts and has invested much in the annual Postgraduate Writers' Conference there. Her most recent publications include *Quiddity* and *Eclipse*.

Mariela Griffor is the author of *The Psychiatrist* (Eyewear Publishing, 2013) and *Exiliana* (Luna Publications, 2007) and *House* (Mayapple Press, 2007). Her translation of Pablo Neruda's *Canto General* is forthcoming from Tupelo Press. She is publisher of Marick Press and Consul for Chile in Michigan, where she lives with her family.

Shannon Elizabeth Hardwick received her MFA from Sarah Lawrence College. The author of a chapbook, *Hummingbird Mind* (Mouthfeel Press), she is an associate poetry editor for *The Boiler Journal*. Her work has appeared in *Salt Hill*, *Versal*, *Sugar House Review*, *Four Way Review*, among others. She writes in the deserts of West Texas.

Janet Ruth Heller is the author of the award-winning children's book about bullying, *How the Moon Regained Her Shape* (Sylvan Dell, 2012); the poetry books *Exodus, Folk Concert: Changing Times,* and *Traffic Stop*; and the scholarly book *Coleridge, Lamb, Hazlitt, and the Reader of Drama* (Missouri, 1990). She is president of the Michigan College English Association.

Phyllis Hoge, now of Albuquerque, taught literature and poetry writing at University of Hawaii, raised four children, and published three chapbooks and five collections of poems, most recently *Hello, House* (Daniel and Daniel, 2012), illustrated by Maxine Hong Kingston. She received the Hawaii Award for Literature in recognition of her poetry and for her founding of the first Poets in the Schools program in America and the University of Hawaii graduate degree in poetry.

Lindsay Illich lives in Milton, Massachusetts. Her work has appeared in *Gulf Coast, Occupoetry, Rio Grande Review, Salamander, Best of Kore Press 2012, Hurricane Blues: How Katrina and Rita Ravaged A Nation*, and *Improbable Worlds: An Anthology of Texas and Louisiana Poets.*

T. J. Jarrett is a writer and software developer in Nashville, Tennessee, and the author of *Ain't No Grave* (New Issues Press, 2013). Jarrett's second collection *Zion* was winner of the Crab Orchard Open Competition and was published by Southern Illinois University Press in 2014.

Brett Elizabeth Jenkins lives and writes in Saint Paul, Minnesota. She is the author of the chapbook *Ether/Ore* (NAP, 2012). Look for her work in *Beloit Poetry Journal, [PANK], Potomac Review, RHINO Poetry, Revolver*, and *Paper Darts.*

Lois P. Jones is host of KPFK radio's Poets Café in Los Angeles and poetry editor for *Kyoto Journal*. Some of her publications include *Narrative Magazine, American Poetry Journal, The Warwick Review*, and *Eyewear*, and her poems have won honors from judges Fiona Sampson and Kwame Dawes, among others. In 2012, she was awarded both the Liakoura and Tiferet poetry prizes.

Laurel Kallen, the author of the poetry collection *The Forms of Discomfort* (Finishing Line Press), is a poet and fiction writer who teaches at the City University of New York. She is a recipient of the Stark Short Fiction Award and the Teacher/Writer Award. Her work has appeared in *Atlanta Review, Portland Review, Devil's Lake, Jabberwock*, and elsewhere.

Joan Naviyuk Kane's *The Cormorant Hunter's Wife* received a 2009 Whiting Writers' Award. *Hyperboreal* won the 2012 Donald Hall Prize. With a recent fellowship from the Rasmuson Foundation, she is the 2014 Indigenous Writer-in-Residence at the School for Advanced Research and a member of the MFA faculty at the Institute for American Indian Arts.

Catherine Keefe is a California poet and essayist. She is the founding editor of *dirtcakes*, a journal dedicated to themes suggested by the United Nations Millennium Goals to end extreme poverty. Her work has recently appeared in *Superstition Review, ArtPrize Anthology*, and *Minerva Rising*. She teaches writing at Chapman University and also facilitates drum circle workshops and guided meditation.

A native of the Southwest, **Janet Kenning** is a past recipient of a Colorado Council on the Arts grant in poetry. Her work has appeared in the literary journals *Ploughshares*, *Diagram*, *Calyx*, *Fine Madness*, and others. She has an MFA from the Writers' Workshop at the University of Iowa.

Molly Sutton Kiefer is the author of the lyric essay *Nestuary* (Richocet Editions, forthcoming) as well as the poetry chapbooks *The Recent History of Middle Sand Lake* and *City of Bears*. More about her work can be found at mollysuttonkiefer.com.

Jen Kindbom is the author of *A Note on the Door* (Finishing Line Press), and *Cadabra* (Cascadia Publishing House, forthcoming). Her poems have appeared in *Literary Mama*, *Perigee*, *Lummox*, and *Connotation Press*, among others. Jen earned her MFA from Ashland University. A native of Cleveland's West Side, she currently resides with her family in Wooster, Ohio.

Alan S. Kleiman is the author of *Grand Slam*, a collection of poems (Crisis Chronicles Press, 2013). His poems have appeared in magazines and anthologies around the world and been translated into many languages. He appeared at the performing art series at Virginia Museum of Fine Arts, and when not writing poetry, works in New York City as an attorney.

David Koehn's first book, *Twine*, won the 2013 May Sarton Prize in Poetry (published by Bauhan Publishing, 2014). He's also the author of *Tunic* (speCt!, 2013), a collection of Catullus translations, and *Coil*, which won the Midnight Sun chapbook contest sponsored by the journal *Permafrost* at University of Alaska.

Jacqueline Kolosov's third collection of poetry is *Memory of Blue* (Salmon, 2014). She has published poetry and creative prose in *Poetry*, *The Southern Review*, *Bellevue Literary Review*, and elsewhere. She is on the creative writing faculty at Texas Tech University and lives with her family in Lubbock.

Rachel Kubie is a public reference librarian in Charlotte, North Carolina. She has had poems in *Mudlark*, *RHINO*, *Sou'wester*, *Potomac Review*, *Rattapallax*, and *Drunken Boat*. She is one of nearly a thousand people arrested in the summer of 2013 in the Moral Monday protests in Raleigh, North Carolina, and is still awaiting a trial date.

Kali Lamparelli received her MFA from Lesley University and is currently working as an executive assistant by day and a freelance writer and poet by night. Her first poetry collection aims to explore the violent oppression of women in today's world.

Kyle Laws's poems, stories, and essays have appeared in magazines for thirty years and have earned four Pushcart nominations. Her collections include *Wildwood* (Lummox Press, 2014), *My Visions Are As Real As Your Movies, Joan of Arc Says to Rudolph Valentino* (dancing girl press, 2013), *George Sand's Haiti* (co-winner of *Poetry West*'s 2012 chapbook award), and *Going into Exile* (Abbey Chapbooks, 2012). She is editor of Casa de Cinco Hermanas Press.

Erika Lutzner's first two chapbooks, *Invisible Girls* and *Bedtime Stories,* were published by dancing girl press, which will publish her *The Delectable Names of Harsh Places* in 2015. Two other books are new: *You Were My Death* (Kattywompus Press, 2014) and *Everything Slipped Away From Me* (Calypso Press, 2015).

Kate Lutzner's poetry has appeared in *The Antioch Review, Rattle,* and *Barrow Street.* She has been featured online in Verse Daily and in Tupelo Quarterly.

Laurin Becker Macios has her MFA in poetry from the University of New Hampshire and is the Program Director for Mass Poetry. She has work published or forthcoming in *[PANK], Theodate, RHINO Poetry, Boxcar Poetry Review,* and elsewhere. She lives in Boston with six plants and one wicked awesome husband.

Barbara March's work has appeared or is forthcoming in the *Denver Quarterly, Words Fly Away: Fukushima Anthology, Written River, Red Rock Review,* and other journals and anthologies. She is the co-founder of the Surprise Valley Writers' Conference and lives in Cedarville, California, where she advocates for poetry in the rural West.

Lea Marshall's work has appeared in *Linebreak, Unsplendid, Hayden's Ferry Review, Diode Poetry Journal,* and elsewhere. She holds an MFA from Virginia Commonwealth University, where she also currently serves as interim chair of the Department of Dance and Choreography.

Charlotte Matthews holds the Maxwell C. Weiner Chair in Humanities at Missouri University of Science and Technology. In addition to her two full-length collections (*Green Stars* and *Still Enough to be Dreaming,* both from Iris Press), her work has recently appeared in *American Poetry Review, Virginia Quarterly Review, Ecotone,* and *Chatauqua.*

J. Kirk Maynard lives in his hometown of Portland, Oregon, with his wife, Jessica, and their dog, Lucy. He received his MFA at the University of Alabama, and his poems and reviews have been published in *Blueline, White Whale Review, Cactus Heart, Kudzu Review,* and *Arch,* among others. His new chapbook is *Throwaways* (MollyDog Press, 2014).

Mike McGeehon lives in Newberg, Oregon. He has worked as a social worker, janitor, and nursing home attendant, and for the past seven years as a teacher for an online charter school. His work is featured in the anthology *Gathered: Contemporary Quaker Poets* (Sundress Publications, 2013) and in a number of journals.

George McKim earned an MFA in painting in 1985. He began writing poetry at the age of fifty-six. His poetry has appeared or is forthcoming in *Dear Sirs, Shampoo, Diagram, elimae, Ditch, Cricket Online Review, BlazeVox,* and *The Found Poetry Review Pulitzer Remix Project.*

Janie Elizabeth Miller is a poet and essayist whose works explore environmental imagination and activism. She teaches poetics at the University of Washington in Tacoma and has completed a collection of poetry, *Under Cleave.* Her poems can be found in *Terrain.org, Poecology, Cura: A Literary Magazine of Art & Activism,* and *Cimarron Review.*

Luisa Muradyan is originally from Ukraine and currently teaches English at Kansas State University. She was recently nominated for a Pushcart Prize for her work in *Ninth Letter*. Previous work has appeared in *Anderbo, A-Minor Magazine, Camroc Press Review*, and *Neon Literary Magazine*.

A native of California, Diana Khoi Nguyen is working on completing her first manuscript in Lewisburg, Pennsylvania. She has poems and reviews in or forthcoming in *Poetry, Lana Turner, Kenyon Review*, and *West Branch*. Website: www.dianakhoinguyen.com

Dan Nowak is the editor of Imaginary Friend Press. He has four collections of poetry.

Richard J. O'Brien lives in Pennsylvania, where he is an adjunct professor of English at Holy Family University; he also teaches at two county colleges in New Jersey. In 2012, he completed his MFA in creative writing from Fairleigh Dickinson University. His poems have appeared in *Stoneboat, New Plains Review, Star*Line*, and other journals.

Calvin Olsen holds an MFA from Boston University, where he was a 2011 Robert Pinsky Global Fellow. His poetry and translations have appeared in *Salamander, New Haven Review, Dialogue, SWAMP*, and the anthology *Fire in the Pasture: Twenty-first Century Mormon Poets* (Peculiar Pages, 2011). He teaches at Boston University.

A graduate of Florida Atlantic University's Creative Writing MFA program, Michael J Pagán's work has appeared in *The Rumpus, DIAGRAM, Pacifica Literary Review, Spork Press, Verse, The Coachella Review, BlazeVOX, Spittoon Magazine, Menacing Hedge*, and *Mad Hatters' Review*. He currently lives in Deerfield Beach, Florida.

Kara Penn lives in Denver, Colorado, with her husband and two small daughters. She works as a consultant with mission-based organizations, and has co-authored *Fail Better: Design Smart Mistakes and Succeed Sooner*, a general management book forthcoming from Harvard Business Review Press (2014). She has published poems in *Meadowlands Review, Ekphrasis*, and *Rockhurst Review*.

K. Alma Peterson is the author of a chapbook, *Befallen* (Propaganda Press, 2009) and a full-length book of poems, *Was There No Interlude When Light Sprawled the Fen* (BlazeVOX Books, 2010). She is a graduate of the Warren Wilson MFA Program for Writers. K. Alma (Kathy) lives in Minnesota and Florida.

Nina Pick holds masters degrees in Comparative Literature from the University of California – Berkeley and in Counseling Psychology from Pacifica Graduate Institute. Her poetry has appeared in the journals *Arion, Written River, Stone Canoe*, and *ISLE*, and in several anthologies. She lives and teaches in northern California.

A native of Kolkata, India, **Kushal Poddar** writes poetry, scripts, and prose. He is the author of *All Our Fictional Dreams* (Lulu, 2010) and his work has been featured in several anthologies in Europe and in America. His forthcoming book is *Kafka Dreamed of Paprika*.

Heidi Johannesen Poon has been supported by fellowships from Brown University, the University of Iowa, the MacDowell Colony, the Virginia Commission for the Arts, and Carlow University. She published her first chapbook *The Good News of the Ground* with the Poetry Society of America in 2009. She lives with her family in Charlottesville, Virginia.

Colin Pope's poetry has appeared or is forthcoming in *Slate*, the *Best New Poets* annual, *The Los Angeles Review*, and *The Texas Review*. Originally from New York, he currently teaches in the English department at Texas State University.

Melissa Reeser Poulin's poems have appeared or are forthcoming in *basalt*, *Catamaran Literary Reader*, *Ruminate*, and *Water-Stone Review*. She is currently editing *Winged*, an anthology of new writing about honey bees, to benefit pollinator conservation (see the website: wingedbook. com).

Bill Prindle was first published in the *Pennsylvania Review* in the 1970s. He finished his manuscript *Heards Mountain Poems* in 2012, and has submitted widely. He is studying advanced poetry writing with Gregory Orr at the University of Virginia and is active in Charlottesville's WriterHouse organization.

Jacey Blue Renner received her MFA from Lesley University. She is married to an Air Force officer, who has been deployed three times. Her first collection hopes to explore the importance of the poetic perspective during war times.

Claudia Rodríguez, is a writer/performer from Compton, California, and she received her MFA in creative writing from the California Institute of the Arts (CalArts). She currently teaches at California State University in Dominguez Hills. She is a founding member of Butchlalis de Panochtitlan (BdP), a sketch-driven performance/installation/video ensemble.

Denise Rodriguez received her MFA in poetry from Texas State University in San Marcos, Texas. Her work has appeared in *Room Magazine*, *A River and Sound Review*, *VAYAVYA Magazine*, *The Doctor T. J. Eckleburg Review*, *Kweli Journal*, and *The Pedestal Magazine*.

William David Ross grew up in the north country of Vermont and thought "the Big Apple" a perfect place to strike out on his own. While in New York City, he earned a MFA from Columbia University in poetry. His current manuscript is called *Among the Rubble Graces*. His writing has appeared in various journals.

Emily R. Rudofsky hails from the Boston area by way of the Mid-Atlantic region. Her first chapbook is *Ravenous* (Yes/No Press, 2014). Her poetry and artwork has appeared in *Oddball Magazine*, *The Gabbler*, *The Fat City Review*, and *ZigZag Folios, Volume 2*.

Lisa Donne Sampson of Plymouth, Massachusetts, attended Tupelo Press's weeklong retreat in Truchas Peaks, New Mexico, in 2012, then in 2013 participated in Tupelo's 30/30 project. In 2012, she published a digital chapbook, *Moon Rose Sun Set*, and a recent poem has been featured in the quarterly journal *Off the Coast*.

Julie (Julianza) Shavin is a composer, poet, and visual artist. Recipient of three grants from Pikes Peak Arts Council, she was named their Performance Poet of the Year in 2011 and Page Poet of the Year in 2012. She currently serves on the council's board of directors. Past president of Poetry West (www.poetrywest.org), she is also an animal-welfare advocate and activist. Website: www.droppinglikerubies.com

M. E. Silverman is founder of Blue Lyra Review and review editor of Museum of Americana. He is author of a chapbook, *The Breath before Birds Fly* (ELJ Publications, 2013). His poems have appeared in over seventy-five journals, including *Crab Orchard Review* and *December*. He recently completed co-editing (with Deborah Ager) *Bloomsbury's Anthology of Contemporary Jewish American Poetry*.

Margie Skelly's poetry manuscript *Whispers from Earth and Heaven* has twice been named among the finalists for the Word Works Washington Prize, and she has been awarded first place in various poetry contests. Living in Chicago, she loves singing with the Edgewater Singers, Chicago Symphony Chorus, and North Shore Choral Society.

Joanna Solfrian is a writer and teacher living in northwestern Connecticut. A MacDowell Fellow, she has been published in various literary magazines, and her first book, *Visible Heavens* (Kent State University Press, 2010), was winner of the 2009 Wick Prize, judged by Naomi Shihab Nye. She is currently working on a novel-in-verse for middle readers.

Readers can find recent poems and stories by **Mattie Quesenberry Smith** in *Avatar*, *Dappled Things*, *Dark Matter Journal*, *Diagram*, *Floyd County Moonshine*, and *Ruminate*. She serves as an instructor at the Virginia Military Institute and at Dabney S. Lancaster Community College, and she lives at the foot of Little House Mountain in Lexington, Virginia.

Katerina Stoykova-Klemer is the author of three poetry books, most recently *The Porcupine of Mind* (Broadstone Books, 2012). She is the founder of poetry and prose groups in Lexington, Kentucky. She hosts Accents, a literary radio show on WRFL, 88.1 FM, in Lexington. In 2010, she launched Accents Publishing.

With an MFA from Queens University in Charlotte, **Charles A. Swanson** taught high school and college English in Gretna, Virginia, and retired in 2012. His two books of poems are *After the Garden* (MotesBooks, 2009), and *Farm Life and Legend* (Finishing Line Press, 2009), and he pastors a small church, Melville Avenue Baptist Church in Danville, Virginia.

Larissa Szporluk is the author of five books of poetry, most recently *Traffic with Macbeth* (Tupelo Press, 2011). An associate professor of English and creative writing at Bowling Green State University, she has received grants from the Guggenheim Foundation and the National Endowment for the Arts.

Dan Thomas-Glass is the author of *Seaming* (Furniture Press, 2010), *The Great American Beatjack, Volume 1* (Perfect Lovers Press, 2012), and *Kate & Sonia (in the months before our second daughter's birth)* (Little Red Leaves Textile Series). He lives in Los Angeles with his wife Kate and their daughters Sonia and Alma.

A. M. Thompson's work has been published in Europe (in *Acumen*, *Staple*, and *Vine Leaves*) and the United States (in *ARDOR*, *Best New Writing 2014*, *Blast Furnace*, *Philosophy After Dark*, *Leopard Seal*, and *Mezzo Cammin*). She lives with her husband and daughter in Washington, D.C., where she edits exams for the American Nurses Credentialing Center. Website: www. wellspringofwords.net

Peter Vanderberg served in the U.S. Navy from 1999 to 2003 and received an MFA from Queens College, City University of New York. His work has appeared in *CURA*, *Ozone Park*, and *Newtown Literary*, and in combination with his brother James's paintings in their book, *Weather-Eye* (Ghostbird, 2011). He teaches at St. John's Preparatory School and Hofstra University.

A farm kid and Fulbright fellow, **Arlo Voorhees** writes trans-fat–free, certifiably organic, exclusively hand-crafted (calluses included) poetry. *Smiling in Photographs*, an animated collaboration of his new manuscript with filmmaker Noah Lambie, premiered in 2014. An MFA alum from the University of Oregon, he edits poetry for *Pilvax* magazine.

Mobi Warren is a middle school math teacher and environmentalist/naturalist in San Antonio, Texas. She is the translator of several books by Vietnamese Buddhist monk Thich Nhat Hanh, including *Fragrant Palm Leaves* (Riverhead, 1999) and *Old Path White Clouds* (Parallax, 1991). Her poems have appeared in regional journals and several anthologies.

Scott Weaver is working on his first book, *Home & Ghosts*. His poems have appeared *Rattle*, *The New York Quarterly*, *DIAGRAM*, *UCity Review*, and other journals. He lives in Austin, Texas, with his wife Kelli Ford and their daughter, Cypress. You can find him on Twitter @scottweaver.

Allyson Whipple is the director of the Austin Feminist Poetry Festival and author of the chapbook *We're Smaller Than We Think We Are* (Finishing Line Press, 2013). She teaches at Austin Community College and is currently at work on her first full-length collection, entitled *Curved Tongue, Forked Road*. She is also pursuing a black belt in kung fu.

Scott Whitaker is the literary review editor for *The Broadkill Review* and is a member of the National Book Critics Circle. He is the author of four chapbooks of poetry. His young adult novel *Seven Days on the Mountain* and short story collection *Toxic Tourism* are available on Kindle from Amazon. He blogs at http://fieldrecord.blogspot.com/.

Katharine Whitcomb is the author of *The Art Courage Program* (Jaded Ibis Press, 2014) and three collections of poems, *Saints of South Dakota & Other Poems* (Bluestem Press, 2000), *Hosannas* (Parallel Press, 1999) and *Lamp of Letters* (Floating Bridge Press, 2009). Website: www.katharinewhitcomb.com/.

M. Clara White lives in Vermont. You can find her work in *NAP Magazine*, *Eunoia Review*, *The Medulla Review*, *Specter*, *Petrichor Machine*, *Stymie Magazine*, *Tupelo Quarterly*, and the *RHINO Poetry* annuals in 2011 and 2012.

Nicholas YB Wong's books of poems are *Cities of Sameness* (Desperanto, 2012) and *Self Split* (forthcoming from Kaya Press). In 2012, he was a finalist for both the New Letters Poetry Award and the Wabash Prize for Poetry.

Margaret Young has two collections of poetry, *Willow from the Willow* (Cleveland State Poetry Center, 2002) and *Almond Town* (Bright Hill Press, 2011). She is currently working on translations of contemporary Argentine poets. She teaches creative writing at Endicott College and lives in Beverly, Massachusetts.

Desmond Kon Zhicheng-Mingdé is the author of *The Arbitrary Sign* (Red Wheelbarrow Books) and *I Didn't Know Mani Was a Conceptualist* (Math Paper Press, 2013). Founder and publisher at Squircle Line Press, he has edited more than ten books and co-produced three audio books. Also an interdisciplinary artist, his commemorative ceramics are in collections in India, the Netherlands, the United Kingdom, and the United States.

Kelleen Zubick's poetry has appeared in a number of journals including *Agni Online*, *Barrow Street*, *Dogwood*, *The Massachusetts Review*, and *Willow Springs*. She earned an MFA in creative writing from Arizona State University and has been awarded artist residencies by the Anderson Center for Interdisciplinary Studies (in Minnesota) and from the Kimmel Harding Nelson Center for the Arts (in Nebraska).

Nina Israel Zucker received her MFA from Columbia University. She has worked for the Geraldine R. Dodge Foundation as a facilitator for the Spring/Fountain poetry series for educators. Her work has appeared in *Poets Against the War*, the *New York Times*, *Philadelphia Stories*, and many journals. She teaches Spanish and English Language Learner (ELL) classes in Cherry Hill, New Jersey.

Other books from Tupelo Press

www.ingramcontent.com/pod-product-compliance
Lightning Source LLC
Chambersburg PA
CBHW021506090426
42739CB00007B/487